Reflection, Refraction, and Resituation of Dabrowski's Theory of Personality

Salvatore Mendaglio, Ph.D.
University of Calgary

Edited by: William D. Beuscher
Interior design: The Printed Page
Cover design: Julee Hutchison

Published by
Gifted Unlimited, LLC
12340 U.S. Highway 42, No. 453
Goshen, KY 40026
www.giftedunlimitedllc.com

© 2024 by Salvatore Mendaglio, Ph.D. & Gifted Unlimited LLC

ISBN: 978-1-953360-31-1

All rights reserved under International and Pan-American Copyright Conventions. Unless otherwise noted, no part of this book may be reproduced, stored in a retrieval system, or transmitted in any form or by any means—electronic, mechanical, photocopying, or otherwise—without express written permission of the publisher, except for brief quotations or critical reviews.

Printed and bound in the United States of America.

Gifted Unlimited and associated logos are trademarks and/or registered trademarks of Gifted Unlimited.

At the time of this book's publication, all facts and figures cited are the most current available. All telephone numbers, addresses, and website URLs are accurate and active; all publications, organizations, websites, and other resources exist as described in this book; and all have been verified as of the time this book went to press. The author(s) and Gifted Unlimited make no warranty or guarantee concerning the information and materials given out by organizations or content found at websites, and we are not responsible for any changes that occur after this book's publication. If you find an error or believe that a resource listed here is not as described, please contact Gifted Unlimited.

*To William "Bill" Tillier for his tireless efforts
to keep his mentor's theory alive.*

Acknowledgments

I find it difficult to capture in words the gratitude that I feel for the people who were closely involved with the process of completing this book. In a way, my part was easy because, once I get myself down to writing, I find the process quite enjoyable, playing with competing ideas. Taking my ideas in draft form and translating them into comprehensible, readable text requires effort by those involved in the publication process.

Barbara, my wife, was the first to make such an effort. Not only did she voice her enthusiasm for my writing this book, but she also demonstrated it by adopting the role of unofficial editor. Her questions and suggestions added clarity and consistency to my expression of ideas. Barbara also bore the brunt of initial copy-editing dealing with numerous remnants of my English-as-a-second-language background. With her efforts, I was able to submit a presentable draft. I am extremely grateful for Barbara's encouragement and practical support.

The editorial staff of Gifted International obviously carefully reviewed my manuscript, as indicated by their provision of valuable feedback. I sincerely appreciated both their suggestions, which added clarity to the expression of my ideas, and their copy-editing, which removed remaining obstacles in the way of the book's readability.

Publisher Molly Isaacs-McLeod, Gifted Unlimited, deserves special thanks because her interest and continuing support for my work added to my motivation to write what you are about to read.

S.M.

Table of Contents

Acknowledgments	v
Prologue	ix
Preface	xi
Part I: The Theory and Me	**1**
Chapter 1. What is the Theory of Positive Disintegration?	3
Chapter 2. Major Constructs of Dąbrowski's Theory of Personality	11
Chapter 3. My Key Psychological Constructs: A Dąbrowskian Perspective	35
Chapter 4. Feeling Bad Can Be Good	45
Part II: Dąbrowskian Development	**51**
Chapter 5. Levels of Development	53
Chapter 6. Emergence of Disintegrating Dynamisms	75
Chapter 7. Emergence of Developmental Dynamisms	97
Part III: Dąbrowskian Constructs in Psychological Context	**107**
Chapter 8. Self	109
Chapter 9. Intelligence	121
Chapter 10. Hierarchy of Values	137
Chapter 11. Mental Health	163
Part IV: Concluding Reflections	**181**
Chapter 12. Modifications and Elaborations	183
References	193
About the Author	199

Prologue

I have a print by Rene Magritte (Belgian surrealist painter) in my office that I have treasured since my graduate student days. The painting is that of a pipe used for smoking tobacco with the caption: *Ceci n'est pas une pipe* (See Figure 1). It is my favorite print and over the years I have found ways of enjoying it (as I am doing now while writing this!).

Figure 1. Rene Magritte's "The Treachery of Images"
© *C. Herscovici/Artists Rights Society (ARS), New York*

One way that I have enjoyed the print has been referring to it in my interactions with graduate students and clients. Graduate students routinely approach professors in search of supervisors for their theses. When I meet with a student who I think is a good academic match (and if I am also in a playful mood), I say: "I will be your supervisor on the condition that you answer a question correctly." Then I direct the student's attention to my Magritte print, asking them whether they understand the French caption. (In Canada, it is not an outlandish question, but it is not *the* question.) If they do not understand it, I translate for them: "This is not a pipe." Then I pose my question: *Why is the caption a correct statement?* Some students do not respond with my correct answer, but I supervise them anyway. I also use the same procedure with some of the gifted children and their parents who I see professionally. It is remarkable how virtually all the young children respond with my correct answer, while their parents leave the office still pondering my question (and perhaps wondering if they chose a competent psychologist).

As it turns out, a great deal has been written about Magritte's paintings, with varying interpretations of their meaning. My "correct" answer (it is not a pipe, it is a painting of a pipe) is, of course, the product of what I know about Rene Magritte and his philosophy of painting, as perceived through the lens of my knowledge of and experience with art. Since I have little knowledge of art, reflecting the adage "I don't know art, but I know what I like," I rely almost exclusively on book knowledge and what little art education I have gleaned in my visits to museums. In a peculiar way, I see a similarity between my understanding of both Magritte's pipe and Dąbrowski's Theory of Positive Disintegration. Both are products of my interpretation using my knowledge of the painter and the theorist and their respective fields of endeavor. However, there is an important difference: my knowledge of Magritte and the field of art is superficial; my knowledge of Dąbrowski's theory and the field of psychology is deeper. While I am more confident in my understanding of Dąbrowski's theorizing than I am of Magritte's painting, I do not pretend to have full comprehension of the theory of positive disintegration. Here are my careful considerations of the theory through the lens of established psychological constructs as well as my academic and psychotherapeutic experience.

Preface

Secondary sources are book-length interpretations of theories, essential for understanding any challenges in the original publication. This is particularly the case with theories that are innovative, questioning the *status quo* in a field of study. There are several examples of this premise in the field of psychology. Prime among such theories is the genetic epistemology of Jean Piaget. There is little doubt that Piaget's theory is a unique explanation of how cognition develops. Many psychologists are, to varying degrees, familiar with Piaget's theory, and we know that attempts to read it in the original prove exceedingly challenging. (That's certainly been the case in my experience!) The knowledge we gathered about Piaget's genetic epistemology was gleaned to a large extent from secondary sources by scholars who patiently read many if not all of Piaget's writings. As a result of this scholarly endeavor, Piaget's theory gained an incredible degree of importance and popularity in psychology and education. An obvious sign of the endurance of his theory is the fact that universities continue to require psychology and education students in undergraduate programs to study Piaget's work, all the more remarkable considering it is originally an old, esoteric philosophical work, in French, from the 1920's. Such popularity could not have been achieved without secondary sources. (I find it difficult to imagine that many students would read Piaget's Biology and Knowledge, published in 1971 by University of Chicago Press). John H. Flavell produced the first major work in English regarding Piaget's theory, The Developmental Psychology of Jean Piaget (1963), and singlehandedly launched the theory into American psychology and education. The rest, as they say, is history.

In my study of Dąbrowski's Theory of Positive Disintegration, the focus of this book, I see some general similarity to Piaget's genetic epistemology. Not conceptually, because Dąbrowski had his disagreements with Piaget's theorizing, but rather with respect to proposing an alternate conceptualization of Piaget's topic of interest, which is human development. Dąbrowski began articulating his theory in the 1930s in Poland. He presented his work in Polish and French publications, with relatively few in English. His English language books present challenges to the reader, though unlike Piaget, we are not confronted routinely with paragraph-length sentences containing several subordinate clauses, requiring inordinate effort to decipher. With Dąbrowski's English we are challenged by the juxtaposition of normally incompatible words ('positive' and 'disintegration' as the most immediate example) as well as the idiosyncratic use of common psychological terms, which often changes the valence associated with the term (e.g., personality is redefined and imbued with positive value). In effect, the theory of positive disintegration requires that readers expend effort, though it is not aimed at deciphering information, but rather at inhibiting the conventional meaning of psychological terms. Were it not for scholars who knew the theory and saw its merits, it would have remained unknown outside of Europe. Scholars associated with the field of gifted education first introduced aspects of the theory.

Since its introduction in the 1970s, a great deal of literature and empirical studies regarding the theory of positive disintegration have been published, but no secondary source appeared until recently. William Tillier's 2018 book is the first secondary source on Dąbrowski's theory. Tillier, one of Dąbrowski's graduate students and archivist of his work, depicts a faithful rendition of the theory. He provides recent research literature that supports Dąbrowski's conceptualizations. Readers familiar with the full breadth of the theory of positive disintegration will likely find that Tillier's treatment is comprehensive, covering all the assumptions, propositions and constructs of the theory. It is important to note that Tillier was not just very familiar with Dąbrowski's

English publications, which describe the theory, but he also had the advantageous opportunity of years of personal contact with Dąbrowski himself. The best secondary sources are those written by authors who know both the theory and the theorist.

During my work, I had Dąbrowski's English books (originally made available by Tillier with the Dąbrowski family permission) which I have studied and referred to since the 1990s. I had the significant advantage, over other authors, of the opportunity to engage in personal conversation with Tillier, my friend and colleague, which was very helpful in clarifying my understanding of the theory. My intense interest in Dąbrowski's theory led to the publication of my edited book (Mendaglio, 2008). Soon after its publication, Tillier pronounced it the best secondary source. Though only part of my book concerned the theory itself, a great deal of it was about its application in gifted education (where the theory currently resides). Tillier's adulation of my book is flattering, but my book is not truly a secondary source.

If you are still reading—many prefaces go unread—I will summarize. I can unequivocally say, based on my view of secondary sources, that this book is not one. I have studied only a fraction of Dąbrowski's publications, the ones in English, and my book does not thoroughly consider the theory of positive disintegration; rather, it focuses only on a selection of constructs that relate directly to personality development.

Dąbrowski's theory has had a profound effect on my thinking about matters psychological. I have been pre-occupied with the theory for many years, initially studying it, and later reflecting on it. I offer my reflections on components of the theory which I have found particularly interesting and challenging. My thoughts have led me to propose clarification of concepts, modifications and additions to the theory. I hasten to add that my suggestions are not inconsistent with the theory: I do not propose an alternate neo-Dąbrowskian perspective.

Intensive thinking about the theory over many years has led to some ideas which I wish I had been able to discuss with the theorist himself. Perhaps he would have enjoyed such a conversation with me, and I hope he would have agreed with my impressions. This book is not a critique of the theory of positive disintegration; it is my celebration of it.

Organization of the Book

Reflections on Dąbrowski's Theory of Personality contains four parts. Part I, the Theory and Me, addresses fundamental issues. Chapter 1 deals with the question of defining Dąbrowski's theory. The main point is that the perception of the theory varies among those familiar with it. Chapter 2 includes the set of selected constructs with which this book is concerned. Chapter 3 contrasts certain psychological constructs, which have been part of my scholarly and psychotherapeutic work, with their meaning in the theory of positive disintegration. Chapter 4 explains a central proposition in Dąbrowski's theory, that negative emotions, under certain conditions, are signs of growth.

Part II deals with conceptualization of development in the theory. Chapter 5 discusses the five levels of development, describing the progression from primitive to exemplary human functioning. Chapter 6 and 7 examine dynamisms that are the forces of development and their emergence in daily living. Chapter 6 discusses disintegrating dynamisms, responsible for the destruction of primitive, self-centered modes of living. Chapter 7 presents the developmental dynamisms, signifying advanced, morally driven modes of living.

Part III, Dąbrowskian Constructs in Context, examines some central constructs of the theory in a broader psychological context. Chapter 8 contrasts Dąbrowski's conception of self with self-concept. Chapter 9 contrasts established theories of intelligence with Dąbrowski's view of intelligence. Chapter 10 compares a hierarchy of values, a concept equated with advanced development, to a social psychological theory of values. Chapter 11 compares Dąbrowski with current conceptions of mental health.

Part IV offers concluding reflections on the theory of positive disintegration. Chapter 12 is a consolidation of reflections appearing in previous chapters, culminating with several suggestions for modification and elaboration of the theory.

Part I
The Theory and Me

Chapter 1. What is the Theory of Positive Disintegration?
Chapter 2. Major Constructs of Dąbrowski's Theory of Personality
Chapter 3. My Key Psychological Constructs: A Dąbrowskian Perspective
Chapter 4. Feeling Bad Can Be Good

Chapter 1
What is the Theory of Positive Disintegration?

If we were to ask Dąbrowski this question, his answer would be: the theory of positive disintegration is my theory of personality. This is clear from his writings. In present day, my answer to the question is: it depends on who you ask, because Dąbrowski's theory, like great art, elicits strong emotional reactions in those who encounter it. Based on such subjective emotions, responses to the question differ. Some people seem awestruck, declaring that the theory of positive disintegration saved their lives, sometimes literally, not just psychologically. These grateful individuals understand the intent of the theory and would echo Dąbrowski's own reference to it (Tillier, 2018). Other people, perhaps a majority of those familiar with the theory, also view it positively because they see it as an explanation for aspects of giftedness, especially the behavior of gifted children. These positively disposed people would probably view the theory, implicitly or explicitly, as either a theory of giftedness, or more likely, a theory of overexcitabilities. On the other hand, some people reject it outright, declaring that other theories should replace its lofty position in the field of gifted education. They decry the prestige of Dąbrowski's theory in the field of gifted education based on the claim that the theory lacks research support.

I fit into none of those groups, but if my initial unfavorable response had persisted, I would be in the latter group. In retrospect, that was due to my limited knowledge. With increased understanding of Dąbrowski's theory, I became an adherent who sees it as a powerful conceptual tool for understanding numerous psychological phenomena.

I must point out that being a devotee does not preclude offering my reflections on the theory. I say *reflections*, rather than interpretations, because my aim is to communicate my thoughtful considerations of the theory. It goes without saying that any commentary on a theory is, by definition, the product of interpretation. *Reflections* is more apt because it accurately represents my journey with the theory. In my studies I have spent countless hours attempting to understand his intended meanings, while contrasting the theory's components with my knowledge of psychological constructs to which the theory refers. My aim is to share the results of my processing, which include what I believe are clarifications and implications of the theory that are well within the bounds of Dąbrowski's intent. Support for my aims is found in his original English language books on the theory. Dąbrowski writes that his theory is incomplete and that further refinements are left to interested parties who find his work important and compelling. My aim in this chapter, and in the entire book, are to clarify and build upon the theory. In this chapter, I present my preliminary answer to the question that I pose in this chapter by contrasting my reply with published depictions of the theory of positive disintegration. The remaining chapters of this book provide a more detailed answer to: What is the theory of positive disintegration?

In reading other authors' and researchers' publications related to positive disintegration, my perspective differs significantly from others' portrayal of the theory. While Dąbrowski himself outlined over 50 novel ideas in his lexicon of the theory, the majority of empirical and nonempirical publications and other resources address only one construct: overexcitability and its five forms. Even though Dąbrowski's Theory of Positive Disintegration is a psychological theory that deals with development and personality, it is well-known only in the field of gifted education, where it is limited largely to his construct of overexcitability.

To illustrate the points of my perspective, I conjured up an imagined study—complete with results and discussion—which readers are encouraged to replicate.

Perceptions of Dąbrowski's Theory of Positive Disintegration: An Imagined Study

Introduction

<u>Rationale for the study</u>: Dąbrowski, a psychologist and psychiatrist, referred to the theory of positive disintegration as his theory of personality. Based on both his professional affiliations and the content of the theory, one would expect that his theory belongs in the psychological domain of personality. It seems to be somewhat obscure except in the field of gifted education, where it is very well known and influential.

<u>Purpose of the study</u>: This qualitative study is designed to investigate whether the theory of positive disintegration is known in the fields of psychology and education, and if it is known, to what extent?

Method

<u>Participants</u> include four groups: psychologists, graduate students in psychology, teachers, and parents.

<u>Data Collection</u>: One interview question was posed: What, if anything, do you know about the theory of positive disintegration?

Results

Qualitative analysis revealed various themes emergent from the analysis of responses by each group of participants, as seen in Table 1.

Table 1. Emergent Themes of the Imagined Study by Participant Groups

Participant Group	Theme
Psychologists	Huh?
Psychology graduate Students	Worried about missing something
Teachers and Parents	What a waste of money!
Teachers and Parents of gifted children	Overexcitabilities!!

> Results indicated that psychologists responded with variations on "nothing" accompanied by quizzical looks. Graduate students in psychology responded similarly, with signs of varying distress, thinking that they have missed something important in their program of studies. Most teachers and parents answered politely, "never heard of it" with facial expressions conveying, "Here's another ivory tower professor wasting taxpayer dollars." Only a subset of teachers and parents provided different responses, those who were teachers and parents of gifted youth, who responded with delight, "five overexcitabilities!"
>
> ### Discussion
> Of the participants, only teachers and parents of gifted youth recognized the theory. However, their knowledge extended to only one of its numerous components.
>
> Conclusion: The theory of positive disintegration is not known where it should be; and, minimally understood where it is.
>
> Implications: More work needs to be done to communicate the relevance of the theory to psychologists, and to convey to those in education who have knowledge of it that it is not merely a theory of overexcitabilities.

Whereas my study is imaginary, the "results" do illustrate the actual status of Dąbrowski's theory. It is virtually unknown in the fields of psychology and general education, and known in a limited way by some researchers, practitioners and parents in gifted education. As a result, the theory has become associated with almost exclusively with *giftedness* and *overexcitability*. Dąbrowski's theory is not a theory of giftedness but rather a theory of personality; overexcitability is only one of numerous concepts that form the theory. Though I disagree with this narrow perspective, in truth, I have a sympathetic attitude toward individuals who view the theory in such a limited fashion. Knowledge of the theory is most likely gleaned by their reading extant empirical research, which focuses exclusively on investigating the relationship of overexcitability and giftedness. Prescriptive literature and websites generally use overexcitability to explain characteristics of gifted youth. I am critical of a narrow depiction of the theory of positive disintegration because its true potential is revealed only when we attempt to comprehend the theory in its entirety.

In addition to my unfavorable view of the current portrayal of the theory in gifted education, I wonder about the appropriateness of Dąbrowski's own depiction of his theory. It may seem strange or arrogant for a self-proclaimed devotee to question a theorist's own designation; however, I do not perceive the theory of positive disintegration as *only* a theory of personality. Dąbrowski stipulates that positive disintegration is the process by which personality is achieved, the basis on which he apparently christened his theory. According to the theory, achievement of personality is rare, suggesting the theory is applicable to a relatively small minority of humanity. However, that is not the total extent of Dąbrowski's theory: it explains the *full range* of human functioning, from the psychopathic to the normal to the exemplary (personality). Strictly speaking, the true breadth of the theory of positive disintegration is not communicated by *theory of personality*; a title such as *theory of human functioning* would accurately reflect its scope.

What do I Think the theory Is?

In general, virtually everything about Dąbrowski's theory is counterintuitive compared to what is accepted in psychology and psychiatry. An important message of the theory, in plain English, is that psychological experiences are not what they seem. Established psychology characterizes with certainty core constructs of the theory: integration is good, disintegration is bad; adjustment is good, maladjustment is bad; positive emotions are good, negative ones bad. In contrast, the theory of positive disintegration deals with probabilities: integrations, disintegrations, and maladjustment may all be good or bad. Whether such phenomena are beneficial depends on the presence or absence of positive disintegration.

I address the nature of the theory more directly by considering it in two domains: academic and practical. In academic terms Dąbrowski proposed a biosociopsychological conceptualization that explains the variety of human functioning observed universally in humanity. He offers a detailed explanation of how biological and societal forces interact to predict various effects on individual psychology. He adds dimensions not normally seen in theories that purport to explain human development, specifically, morality. Positive disintegration creates a developmental trajectory that, if completed, creates personality, which is characterized by positive values and motivation for moral living. Developmental trajectory is a twofold process: destruction of primitive ways of thinking and behaving, and their replacement by higher forms. The destruction phase creates intense emotional pain which can propel individuals to higher moral ways of being. The absence of positive disintegration, more commonly leads to a life of unquestioning conformity to social norms, or, less often, to one characterized by egocentrism, and possibly, by sociopathic functioning.

In practical terms, positive disintegration is a theory that has a powerful effect on people who encounter it. Perhaps captivated by its title, they are drawn to learn more about it. The theory often has the effect of helping such people understand lifelong experiences that were otherwise inexplicably disturbing. It provides explanations for distressing experiences that have therapeutic effects gained by simply reading even snippets of it. Simply by reading snippets of it, people have experienced therapeutic effects for distressing life experiences. I know of the beneficial effects not only through published accounts, but also through personal and professional contacts. I suspect the powerful effects are produced in people who have a strong desire to understand their experiences, especially those experiences that produce negative emotions. Distress is difficult enough to deal with; not knowing the reasons for it can make it unbearable. Dąbrowski's theory provides a compelling, though counterintuitive, explanation for periods of anxiety and depression to people who are otherwise functioning and, in fact, may be very successful by societal standards. In the context of counseling and psychotherapy, the process of reaping benefits from simply reading accounts of the theory is a form of bibliotherapy.

You would think that a theory with such a powerful effect would be in the mainstream of psychology and of popular culture. As a theory of personality that explains the full range of human functioning, it belongs in the domain of personality psychology. However, the theory is virtually unknown in psychology, having been relegated to the field of gifted education. While this may seem a minor point, it is an important one. Though the theory has implications for the study of giftedness, interest in the theory lies in attempts to understand giftedness through its lens. On the other hand, if accepted in the field of psychology, positive disintegration would likely be considered in the tradition of grand theories of personality, such as those of Freud and H. S. Sullivan, who proposed comprehensive theories of personality development. In that scenario, Dąbrowski's constructs would be portrayed in a fulsome manner and possibly be subjected to empirical investigation. Positioned in gifted education, its utility lies in its applicability to describe, if not explain, aspects of giftedness—under use of a powerful tool.

The theory of positive disintegration is better known in Europe: Dąbrowski published extensively in his native Polish language as well as in French. English was his fifth language. We can speculate that his limited publication record in English North America may be due in part to his need for assistance in producing academic works in English. Books on his theory published in English are merely a fraction of the number of his European publications. Whether Dąbrowski himself or contemporaries submitted manuscripts on the theory to American journals, I suspect the sheer novelty of the theory could have been a reason for rejection.

Kazimierz Dąbrowski created a theory of personality that has the power to shake the foundations of psychology and psychiatry. His theory of positive disintegration not only challenges the concepts of these fields, but also proposes a novel and challenging perspective on taken-for-granted ideas. Unlike other theories of personality, which tend to simply describe processes, Dąbrowski's theory *explains* the processes by which personality develops. As such, his theory provides us with a genuinely new lens through which to see human development and mental health.

CHAPTER 2
Foundational Concepts of Dąbrowski's Theory of Personality

Dąbrowski's theory consists of over fifty discrete concepts which are defined and fused into a coherent whole (Dąbrowski, 1973). Though I will not engage all of the aspects of his theory, comprehensive treatments of it are extant in academia (e.g., Tillier, 2018, Mendaglio, 2008). To select concepts from his theory for discussion in this book, I followed Dąbrowski's own depiction of his theory as a theory of personality, "personality" in the Dąbrowskian sense as the apex of human development. Therefore, the criterion for selecting the concepts is their relationship to the achievement of personality, that is, an advanced stage of human development. With this focus on positive human development, concepts such as one-sided development, negative developmental potential, negative maladjustment, and negative disintegration are less relevant.

My approach in this book is to offer my own understanding of and commentary on the theory of positive disintegration, not to be a review of literature on that theory.

Another preliminary matter relates to the presentation of concepts in the original sources. Dąbrowski's style of writing is in the European intellectual tradition, which favors abstract representation of ideas with little or no provision of examples to clarify their meanings. In present day scholarly writing in psychology, we expect, for example, clear definition of terms when they are first mentioned in an article, as well as examples to illustrate their meanings—especially if a term is new, or if it is a new usage of an old term. Also, definition of terms is expected to be presented in a concise explicit manner. Reading European style literature that has been translated into English with a late 20th/ early 21st century literary mindset poses challenges.

Jason Aronson, in his introduction to Dąbrowski's first English language book (Dąbrowski, 1964) writes a more detailed commentary on the shortcomings of the European style when the intended audience consists of American psychiatrists and psychologists. Aronson's critique can be summed up: *loved the ideas; critiqued the style.* To put this in perspective, we need to realize that by the time Aronson encouraged Dąbrowski to publish in English, Dąbrowski already had an established publication record in Polish and French language academic literature. Neither comments by Aronson nor me should be taken as a criticism of Dąbrowski's work. It is simply a matter of fact that the clash of traditions in scholarly writing poses a challenge for North Americans interested in achieving a full understanding of the theory of positive disintegration.

Because Dąbrowski's numerous concepts are fused into a coherent whole, they are interrelated such that it is difficult to discuss each concept without reference to the others. As a result, a certain of amount of repetition is inevitable.

Dąbrowski's Entangled Concepts

Multilevelness is the innovative lens through which Dąbrowski views the variety of human development. Multilevelness also describes the richness and multi-dimensional experience of reality that characterizes some, but not all, individuals. *Developmental potential* explains the differences among individual experiences of external and internal reality. *Overexcitability* is the main component of developmental potential. *Positive disintegration* is the process of development made possible by sufficient developmental potential. Positive disintegration consists of a dual process: disintegration or destruction of lower forms of thinking and behaving and replacing them with higher forms. *Dynamisms,* which emerge from the five forms of overexcitability, operationalize positive disintegration. They are the mechanisms by which advanced development is attained. Advanced development is the highest form of human development. Personality is the most distinguishing feature of advanced development. Higher and lower mental functioning, a multilevel view of development, is rooted in the hierarchical nature of the central nervous system.

Multilevelness

The foundation upon which Dąbrowski's theory of personality development is based is not positive disintegration but rather *multilevelness*, which permeates the entire theory. The importance of multilevelness cannot be overstated: without it, the theory of positive disintegration would be just another theory of human development. Multilevelness is a paradigm shift in approach to understanding human behavior. At its core, it represents Dąbrowski's observation that human functioning ranges from lower to higher, with respect to complexity and morality.

The idea of a range of mental functioning is a theme central to the theory of positive disintegration—the very concept of development is defined in terms of a progression from lower to higher functioning. Dąbrowski argues that the hierarchical nature of mental functioning is supported by human anatomy, specifically in the structure of the central nervous system as illustrated in Figure 2.

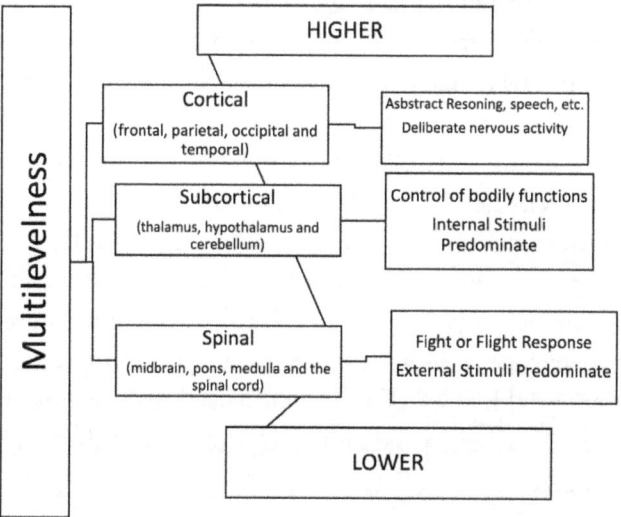

Figure 2. Central Nervous System Hierarchical Structure as Basis for Multilevelness

Subcortical and spinal areas control bodily functions and the fight or flight (or freeze) response—lower levels of functioning. Cortical regions are responsible for higher levels of functioning including abstract reasoning and speech.

> *In this way different parts of the nervous system are concerned with functions that are distinguished as higher or lower. Thus, cortical activities are higher than spinal and subcortical activities. In the cortex the frontal activities are higher than the parietal, occipital and temporal activities.*
> (Dąbrowski, 1970, p. 101)

According to Dąbrowski, the connection between higher and lower levels of functioning in relation to different parts of the nervous system provides empirical basis for the application of this multilevelness to higher and lower levels of mental functioning.

Whether mental functioning is lower or higher depends on which part of the nervous system is activated, which in turn determines behavior. With respect to the connection of levels of central nervous system functioning and correlative levels of behavior, Dąbrowski was influenced by the work of psychiatrist Jan Maurkiewicz, who was Dąbrowski's medical professor (Tillier, 2018). Dąbrowski (1970) cites Maurkiewicz's principle: "the role of external stimuli diminishes as higher levels of the nervous system are involved in the formation of a response" (p. 101). Activities of the spinal part of the nervous system are almost entirely controlled by external stimuli. Activities of the subcortical part are controlled by internal physiological stimuli. At the cortical level, there is a third type of nervous activity that is neither a reaction to external stimuli nor a response to internal organs. Dąbrowski referred to the activity of the cortical part of the brain as deliberate nervous activity, which is not simply a response to present stimuli: "Deliberate nervous activity draws upon the totality of the inscribed experiential history of an individual. Thus, it is not only a response to stimuli actually present, but also to stimuli that acted in the past (recorded experience)" (p. 102).

Dąbrowski proposed the concept of multilevelness because he believed that established psychology could not adequately explain human mental development:

> *Due to the specific nature of mental development in man which consists of the transition from lower, automatic, and rigidly organized mental structures and functions to higher, creative, self-controlled, and authentic forms of mental life-developmental psychology is unable to give a satisfactory account of this process without the use of the concept of multilevelness* (Dąbrowski, 1973, p. ix).

From a Dąbrowskian perspective, influential paradigms of his time, behaviorism, and psychoanalysis, would be considered unilevel, rather than multilevel because they do not differentiate human development into the qualitatively different levels he observed in individuals. Furthermore, established psychological theories could not explain how certain individuals can transcend stimulus-response bonds and biological instincts to a morally high level of development. Dąbrowski, through his concept of multilevelness, explains the multi-dimensionality of human development.

The quality of mental functioning itself is at the root of the varying levels of development. A multilevel view of mental functioning is reflected in individuals' differential experience of reality:

> *By multilevelness of reality we mean external and internal reality of various levels conceived by means of sensory perception, imagination, intellectual, intuitive, or combined operations. Perception of the various levels of reality depends on the kind and level of receptors and transformers of an individual* (Italics added, p. 5).

Experience of reality depends on the level of mental functioning. Experience of reality based solely or mainly on sensory perception will be qualitatively different than when other mental operations are part of the experience. In primitive mental functioning, experience of reality is narrowly limited to the processing of information gleaned from the senses; in more complex mental functioning, experience is broader, enriched by operation of other mental functions, such as imagination. Take for example an encounter with a homeless person. Some individuals will see a disheveled, unclean person who "should get cleaned up and get a job". Others may use similar behavioral descriptors but are more sympathetic and may give a donation. Another set of individuals also see the outward appearance of the person, but they add other dimensions. With strong empathy they wonder: How did the person became homeless? What was the person's occupation? How do this person and other homeless people manage to live day to day? Speculation may include the social forces that might have been involved, society's responsibility, and so on. All three groups of individuals encounter the same external reality but their experience of it is different. Higher levels of mental functioning create a sense of multilevelness in reality, but it is not reality that is multilevel, it is the mental functioning at a higher level that is able to define a more complex reality. It is not reality that is multilevel; it is mental functioning.

Multilevelness is a new principle of development that reflects Dąbrowski's observation that human development ranges from lower to higher forms of mental functioning. Multilevelness also explains differences in the experience of reality, from simple perception of it to an active construction of it. Dąbrowski was motivated to explain the differences in the quality of development that he observed directly in the lives of his patients and people in general; and, indirectly through reading biographies of historical figures. Multilevelness is Dąbrowski's explanation for the diverse forms of development observed in humanity: from psychopathic to normal to exemplary. While multilevelness is a principle of development—a new lens through which to understand the diversity of human development—the level of mental functioning is the mechanism responsible for a particular type of development. A causal relationship exists between mental functioning and level of development; the higher the mental functioning the higher level of development. Mental functioning, itself, is multilevel in nature.

While Dąbrowski notes that multilevelness is an essential lens to view human mental development, it does not explain how differences in mental functioning arise. To account for the multilevelness of mental functioning he observed in people, Dąbrowski determined that a new concept was necessary (Dąbrowski, 1996).

Developmental Potential

To explain the production of different levels of mental functioning, Dąbrowski proposed another new concept to psychology: *developmental potential.*

> *In order to account for differences in the extent of development we introduce the concept of the developmental potential.... The developmental potential is the original endowment which determines what level of development a person may reach if the physical and environmental conditions are optimal.* (Italics in original; Dąbrowski, 1996, p. 10).

Dąbrowski (1972) further defines developmental potential in his glossary of terms as:

> *The constitutional endowment which determines the character and the extent of mental growth possible for a given individual. The developmental potential can be assessed on the basis of the following components: psychic overexcitability, special abilities and talents, and autonomous factors (notably the Third factor).* (p. 253)

The major component of developmental potential is *overexcitability*. It is a heritable property of the central nervous system that significantly alters the quality of experience. Overexcitability has five forms: sensual, psychomotor, intellectual, imaginational, and emotional. Overexcitability is one of the few Dąbrowskian concepts that is very well known, with numerous descriptions readily available in publications and on websites related to giftedness. In my view, some of these representations of overexcitability are inconsistent with Dąbrowski's depiction of them. For clarity, I think it is best to have them described by the theorist's own words:

- **Sensual** overexcitability is a function of a heightened experiencing of sensory pleasure. It manifests itself as need for comfort, luxury, esthetics, fashions, superficial relations with others, frequent changes of lovers, etc. As with the psychomotor form it also may, but need not be, a manifestation of a transfer of emotional tension to sensual forms of expression of which the most common examples are overeating and excessive sexual stimulation. In children sensual overexcitability manifests itself as a need for cuddling, kissing, clinging to mother's body, early heightened interest in sexual matters, showing off, and need to be with others all the time.

- **Psychomotor** overexcitability is a function of an excess of energy and manifests itself, for example, in rapid talk, restlessness, violent games, sports, pressure for action, or delinquent behavior. It may either be a "pure" manifestation of the excess of energy, or it may result from the transfer of emotional tension to psychomotor forms of expression such as those mentioned above.

- **Imaginational** overexcitability in its "pure" form manifests itself through association of images and impressions, inventiveness, use of image and metaphor in verbal expression, strong and sharp visualization. In its "impure" form emotional tension is transferred to dreams, nightmares, mixing of truth and fiction, fears of the unknown, etc. Imaginational overexcitability leads to an intense living in the world of fantasy, predilection for fairy and magic tales, poetic creations, or invention of fantastic stories.

- **Intellectual** overexcitability in contrast to the first three does not distinctly manifest the transfer of emotional tension to intellectual activity under specific forms. This does not mean that intellectual and emotional processes of high intensity do not occur together. They do, but they do not appear to take on such distinct forms. Intellectual overexcitability is manifested as a drive to ask probing questions, avidity for knowledge, theoretical thinking, reverence for logic, preoccupation with theoretical problems, etc.

○ **Emotional** overexcitability is a function of experiencing emotional relationships. The relationships can manifest themselves as strong attachment to persons, living things, or places. From the developmental point of view presented here intensity of feelings and display of emotions alone are not developmentally significant unless the experiential aspect of relationship is present. This distinction is very important. For example, when a child is refused candy, he may throw a temper tantrum just to show his anger. Or he may go away sad thinking he is not loved. (Paragraph formatting added; Dąbrowski, 1996, p. 72-73)

Dąbrowski stipulates that all five forms are necessary to achieve advanced development, however, not all forms are of equal value. This is the case in part because sensual and psychomotor are considered lower forms, while intellectual, imaginational, and emotional are higher forms. To emphasize this point, Dąbrowski states that when only sensual and psychomotor exist in their raw form, combined with high intelligence and ambition, the result can be disastrous for society. He identified Hitler and Stalin as examples of that profile. When all five forms are present, the higher forms, also called by some as the *big three*, serve to transform the raw lower forms—the boundless energy of psychomotor is harnessed for higher aims; hedonism of sensual is transformed into appreciation of visual arts and nature.

It is worthwhile drawing attention to two forms of overexcitability, psychomotor and emotional, that at times are misunderstood. Psychomotor has been used to reframe gifted children's diagnosis of ADHD. For example: "It's not ADHD, it is psychomotor overexcitability", implying that psychomotor overexcitability is wholly positive in nature. However, from Dąbrowski's own description of psychomotor (see p. 27), it can be seen that, in addition to the neutral aspect of boundless energy, there are dark sides to this low form of overexcitability. Emotional overexcitability, when misunderstood, tends to be equated with emotional intensity alone; but understanding it depends on seeing the dynamic within the context of relationships. As an Italian-born Canadian, I am fond of saying that, if emotional overexcitability referred only to emotional intensity, then Italians would have emotional overexcitability. As can be seen from Dąbrowski's descriptions of overexcitability, there is no advantage to replacing ADHD with psychomotor; and the concept of relationships is the defining context of the emotional form.

In addition to overexcitability, developmental potential includes two other components. *Special abilities and talents*, as the phrase implies, includes exceptional abilities in areas such as mathematics and music, which may be apparent in early childhood. *Autonomous forces* (most notably *the Third Factor*) is an allusion to the pivotal theoretical component of *dynamisms*, forces that are essential for the developmental process. While the appearance of certain dynamisms signals the beginning of the process of development, the Third Factor is a super dynamism which indicates the advent of advanced development.

A tripartite definition of developmental potential—overexcitability, special abilities and talents, and third factor—might suggest that it is composed of distinctive parts, which combine to form the potential. This impression is reinforced by Dąbrowski's stating that developmental potential may be assessed by all three components leading to two possible assessments as depicted in Figure 3.

A. Developmental potential = overexcitability + special abilities and talents + autonomous factor
B. Level of Developmental potential is a function of overexcitability OR special abilities and talents OR autonomous factor.
Note: A refers to additive assessment in which all components combine to constitute the potential; B refers to a unitary assessment in which any one of the components may designate the potential.

Figure 3. Two assessments of the Composition of Developmental Potential

However, when I consider the three components in the broader context of the theory of positive disintegration, I wonder whether all three components are actually needed to define developmental potential. Dąbrowski himself identifies overexcitability as the main component of developmental potential. Upon reflection, it may be that overexcitability is not only the most important component, it may be the only one. From this stance, it is conceivable that there is a cause-and-effect relationship among the components—overexcitability is the cause, and special abilities and the autonomous forces are the effects, as represented by Figure 4.

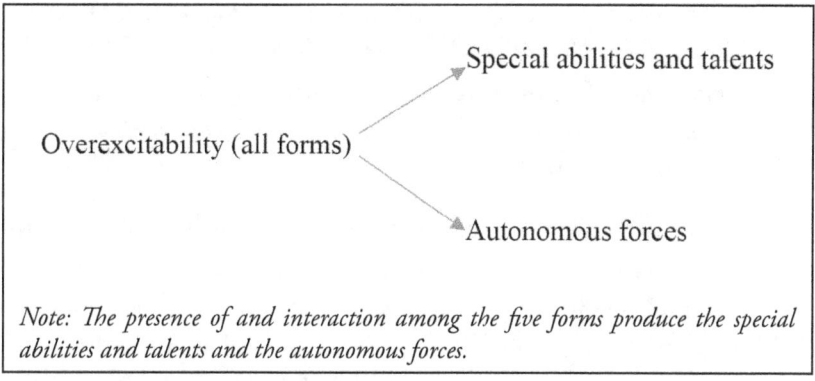

Note: *The presence of and interaction among the five forms produce the special abilities and talents and the autonomous forces.*

Figure 4. Overexcitability as the Sole Component of Developmental Potential

By its transformative effect on mental functioning, it is overexcitability that enables the production of great works of art, music, and profound humanitarianism. The "autonomous forces" of the definition, known as dynamisms, required for advanced development emerge from overly excitable individuals' interactions with the social environment. Overexcitability is the developmental endowment that make activation of dynamisms possible.

> *The five forms of overexcitability undergo extensive differentiation in the course of development. One of its products are developmental dynamisms, i.e., the intrapsychic factors which shape and direct development. Emotional and imaginational overexcitability, in cooperation with the intellectual play the most significant role in their formations possible.* (Dąbrowski, 1996, p. 16)

It is important to recall that Dąbrowski proposed developmental potential to explain his unique paradigm of human development: multilevelness. It is overexcitability that Dąbrowski explicitly uses to explain differences in mental functioning that lead to differential experience of reality:

> [O]ne who manifests a given form of overexcitability, and especially one who manifests several forms of over-excitability, sees reality in a different, stronger, and more multi-sided manner. Reality for such an individual ceases to be indifferent but affects him deeply and leaves long lasting impressions. Enhanced excitability is thus a means for more frequent interactions and a wider range of experiencing. (Dąbrowski, 1972, p.7)

Multilevel experience of external and internal reality is dependent on the presence of "enhanced" overexcitability, usually meaning the presence of all five forms. Dąbrowski explains the multilevelness of development by overexcitability, the paramount element of developmental potential. He explains the process of development by positive disintegration.

Positive Disintegration

> Positive disintegration is deceptively simple to describe: It is Dąbrowski's principle of development that embodies the movement from lower primitive ways of thinking and behaving to higher advanced forms. Lower forms are destroyed—disintegration—and replaced with higher forms—reintegration. Dąbrowski provides the following definition: "**Positive** or developmental **disintegration** effects a weakening and dissolution of lower-level structures and functions, a gradual generation and growth of higher levels of mental functions, and culminates in personality integration. (Boldface in original, Dąbrowski, 1970, pp. 165-166). Elsewhere, Dąbrowski states: "In this book [Dąbrowski, 1970], the term positive disintegration will be applied in general to the process of transition from lower to

higher, broader and richer levels of mental functions. This transition requires a restructuring of mental functions." (Dąbrowski, 1970, p. 18).

In essence, positive disintegration means the destruction of a relatively unreflective compliant mode of living and replacing it with a more reflective, autonomous mode, as represented in Figure 5. It is worth emphasizing that the higher modes of thinking and behaving do not build upon or emerge from the lower forms—lower forms are destroyed. Figure 5 is a schematic representation of the concept of positive disintegration. Development through positive disintegration occurs as the result of many, perhaps countless cycles of destruction of lower forms and replacement by higher forms of thinking and behaving.

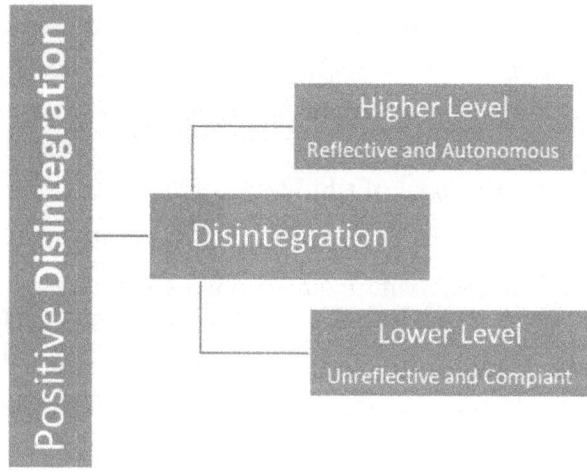

Figure 5. Positive Disintegration: Destruction of Lower Replacement with Higher Forms

While positive disintegration, as a theoretical principle, seems logical once explained, the expected negativity in the word 'disintegration' may lead psychologists to avoid exploring the theory. Dąbrowski himself was aware that juxtaposing positive and disintegration would strike readers as paradoxical due to the meaning of 'disintegration'.

> *Disintegration involves loosening, dissociation, and even breakdown of the structure and organization of psychic functions. The notion of disintegration is in fundamental*

> *opposition to the concept integration which implies unification, organization, and coordination. It seems that the expression positive disintegration is per se paradoxical. This is due to the fact that the standard use of the term "disintegration" has implied abnormality, emotional disturbance. and mental illness. At the same time integration has meant normality, mental development, and absence of disturbance.* (Dąbrowski, 1970, p. 17).

As an aside: In contrast to the dispassionate acknowledgement of the paradoxical nature of positive disintegration, we gain a glimpse into the emotional toll on Dąbrowski for creating such juxtapositions, buried in the Preface of his 1970 book:

> *The main difficulty in the writing of this book was associated with the necessity of giving up most of the traditional, well-elaborated concepts and approaches. Among the usual practical consequences of such an approach is animosity, silence, violent criticism, and even obstacles in research at certain places.* (Dąbrowski, 1970, p. xi)

Positive disintegration is a principle describing development, rather than a mechanism, and this is seen in Dąbrowski's comparison of it with Piaget's concept of *equilibration* (See Table 2). Equilibration may be defined as "the critical process whereby the individual's system of mental actions and operations are reorganized into a new, more advanced structure (Kuhn, 1979, p. 352). As Dąbrowski notes: "One could review and compare the contrasting features of equilibration and of positive disintegration. But then, we would be arguing the merits and uses of different descriptive principles.... (Dąbrowski, 1996, p. 12).

Table 2. Piagetian and Dąbrowskian Principles and Processes of Development

Theorist	Principle	Mechanisms
Piaget	Equilibration	Assimilation & Accommodation
Dabrowski	Positive Disintegration	Dynamisms

Dąbrowski's point is that principles are not sufficient for a theory of human development: it is not sufficient to state that equilibration or positive disintegration describes the process by which development proceeds from one level to another. It is necessary to identify factors that flow conceptually from the principle and are responsible for development. For Piaget, the mechanisms of equilibration are accommodation and assimilation; in contrast, Dąbrowski identifies *dynamisms* as the mechanisms of positive disintegration. Some readers may bristle at my referring to dynamisms as "mechanisms." Actually, Dąbrowski himself uses the term with reference to positive disintegration, for example "fundamental mechanisms of multilevel disintegration". In addition, his 1967 book contains numerous references to mechanisms (Dąbrowski, 1967, e.g., p. 117). In the later works, *mechanism* is replaced by *dynamism*.

Dąbrowski identifies *positive disintegration* as a principle, and *dynamisms* as mechanisms; however, in the context of *development*, they are entangled concepts, difficult to discuss separately. Positive disintegration is development; dynamisms are development.

Dynamisms

Dynamisms are defined as: "Biological or mental forces controlling behavior and its development. Instincts, drives and intellectual processes, combined with emotions, are dynamisms" (Dąbrowski, 1972, p. 294). In addition, Dąbrowski notes that dynamisms are intrapsychic forces affecting development. One interpretation of the definition is that dynamisms are forces that control *all types* of development, not only the type associated with positive disintegration. A careful reading of his texts suggests to me that Dąbrowski often uses *developmental dynamisms* to refer to the autonomous forces active in positive disintegration that are responsible for advanced development.

In my discussion of dynamisms over the years, I use the term "developmental, differently than does Dąbrowski. To express the principle of positive disintegration, I have used *disintegrating* and *developmental* to distinguish the dynamisms implicit in the two phases of positive disintegration: destruction of lower forms of mental function (disintegration), and their replacement with higher forms (development).

Positive disintegration involves destruction of lower forms of mental functioning in the first phase, and a replacement of them with higher forms, a reintegration at a higher level, in the second phase.

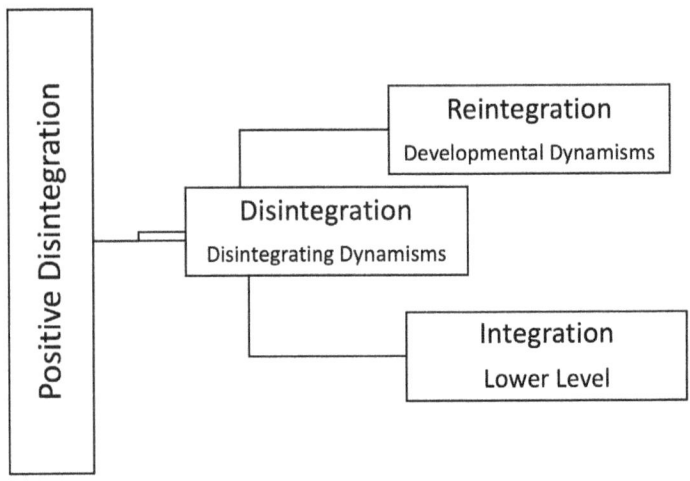

Figure 6. Positive disintegration and dynamisms

Dynamisms are operational in both phases. For the dynamisms of the destructive phase, I use the descriptor *disintegrating*, and for those forming reintegration, I use *developmental*. The combined action of the two types of dynamism "operationalizes" positive disintegration: disintegrating dynamisms destroy lower forms of functioning; developmental dynamisms replace the lower with higher forms of functioning.

Both types of dynamism emerge from the full complement of overexcitability: they are the mature forms of the embryonic autonomous forces that form part of developmental potential. The appearance disintegrating dynamisms signals the beginning of the process of development.

Development

Unlike *positive disintegration* and *dynamism,* which are terms unique to Dąbrowski's theory, *development* is ubiquitous in general psychology. In fact, the concept is as old as the field of modern psychology itself. Two of the most recognized contributions to psychology deal with development: Freud's psychoanalysis and Piaget's genetic epistemology. While their domains are different—Freud's focus is personality development; Piaget's is cognitive development—they have three matters in common. Both are stage theories in which individuals proceed from a lower, primitive stage to a higher, advanced stage. The stages proceed in an invariant, linear sequence, with upper stages build on previous ones. In both theories, individuals progress through some, if not all the stages. Some level of *development*—progression from a lower stage to one or more higher stages—occurs. A final similarity is that of valuation: to my knowledge neither Freud nor Piaget injects values in their stage theories. People at the highest stage in the respective theories are better adjusted (Freud's genital stage) or better thinkers (Piaget's formal operations stage) but they cannot be described as morally better human beings. These similarities between two theories dealing with diverse domains are evident in the perspective of *development* in general psychology. Development—physical, mental, social—tends to occur in hierarchical stages, with higher stages emerging from previous ones. Development, in established theories, is viewed as a universally experienced phenomenon to at least some degree. For example, many but not all individuals reach the stage of formal operations, though it is likely that most people move from the sensorimotor stage to the concrete operations stage, with respect to cognitive development. In this context, we can say that virtually everyone develops cognitively, except for individuals with severe brain anomalies or damage.

A major difference from other theories of development is that Dąbrowski's theory allows for the absence or lack of human development. Development, as the progression from a lower level of mental functioning to a higher level, with all of its ramifications, occurs through positive disintegration and the actions of its dynamisms. Inheritance of sufficient developmental potential is necessary for positive disintegration to occur. Without developmental potential, Dąbrowskian development cannot occur. The amount and intensity of developmental potential determines the level of development that can be achieved. With limited amount of the potential, other types of human development are the result.

The role of developmental potential, particularly the presence or absence of the "autonomous forces"—the dynamisms—component, is evident in Dąbrowski's description of three types of development. The conceptual bases for the types of development are Dąbrowski's factors of development, which I present before describing development types.

Factors of Development. Dąbrowski proposed that development may be controlled by one, two or three factors. The first factor is biology—heredity and constitutional endowment. The second factor is environment. The third factor consists of *autonomous forces*, that is, dynamisms. While the first two factors require little explanation, the third is notably more complex.

> *If heredity may be called the first and environment the second factor, it is necessary to take into consideration the activity of a third factor, i.e., all the autonomous forces. What is their source? How are they developed? What is their genesis? Such questions are difficult to answer. We can only suppose that the autonomous factors derive from hereditary developmental potential and from positive environmental conditions; they are shaped by influences from both. However, the autonomous forces do not derive exclusively from heredity and environment but are also determined by the conscious development of the individual himself.* (Dąbrowski, 1970, p. 34)

The dynamisms, denoted as the third factor, emerge from the full complement of overexcitability. Presence of the five forms of overexcitability indicate a high level of inherited developmental potential.

The three factors create distinct types of human development.

Types of Development. In Dąbrowski (1970) types of development are presented as: *normal, biological, one-sided,* and *autonomous*. In Dąbrowski (1996) *normal* is the most common type; the biological factor is a negative form of *one-sided* development; and autonomous is replaced by *universal or accelerated* development. In the description of the three types presented below, the latter term is used, rather than autonomous. It is worth noting that "advanced development," the most familiar phrase that we interpreters of the theory tend to use, is absent.

Normal development is defined by Dąbrowski (1996) as the most frequently occurring type of development, whose main characteristic is actually a lack of development, devoid of positive growth. Normal development is the result of the dual control by the first and second factors, by biology and environment.

> *By [normal development] we mean a type of development which is most common, and which entails the least amount of inner conflict and of psychological transformation. Development is limited to the maturational stages of human life and to the innate psychological type of the individual. (p. 20)*

Dąbrowski (1970) adds several characteristics to describe normal development. It is biologically determined and organized in a rigid manner, associated with an average level of intellectual functioning and emotional underdevelopment. A key characteristic is adjustment to the norms and values of the external environment. There may be occasional signs of maladjustment to the demands of the social environment, but this is the result of passing maturational milestones (e.g., puberty), or experiencing a distressing social environment event (e.g., loss of employment); adjustment returns once these experiences end.

One-sided development consists of two sub-types that I describe as negative and positive. Negative one-sided development, formerly termed "biological," is manifested by paranoia and psychopathy. If we apply the concept of development as a synonym for positive disintegration, it seems clear that this negative form of development is, in reality, a complete lack of development:

> *...mental processes and structures are strongly "integrated" and resistant to environmental influence. Intelligence serves to manipulate objects in the environment, including, and foremost, other human beings. Combined with good or even great intelligence such integrated structure produces criminal leaders and dictators of whom Hitler and Stalin are the most tragic examples.* (Dąbrowski, 1996, p. 21)

Positive one-sided development results from the predominance of "special abilities and talents" combined with limited overexcitability. The endowment of special abilities and talents is manifested in creativity and productivity in socially prized domains such as painting, literary works, performing arts, and sciences. With respect to overexcitability, intellectual and imaginational functioning are often highly developed, while emotional functioning is often underdeveloped. I describe this type of one- sided development as positive because it represents partial Dąbrowskian development.

Universal or accelerated (autonomous) development. In this context, "universal" is a synonym of *global*, in contrast to partial development. This highest form of development is the product of all the components of developmental potential, with all five forms of overexcitability present in great magnitude, combined with the autonomous factors. Implicit in accelerated development is positive disintegration.

> *Such development manifests strong and multiple forms of overexcitability. But above all it distinctly manifests the individual's awareness and conscious engagement in his own development. Here the autonomous developmental factors carry out the most extensive process of psychic transformation. Development proceeds fairly uniformly although not without intense crises, on a global front encompassing all functions and all dynamisms. (p. 22)*

Factors and Types of Development. The types of development correspond with the factors of development (See Table 3). Negative one-sided development is controlled by the first factor, biology, to which intelligence is subservient. Normal and positive one-sided development are controlled by the combination of the first factor biology, and the second factor, environment. In these two types, the third factor, expressed in autonomous forces or dynamisms, may appear but is not strong enough to motivate further development.

Accelerated development is controlled mainly by the third, autonomous, factor. In the process of this highest form of development, the third factor creates conflict: accelerated development "proceeds in opposition and conflict with the first and second factor" (p.22).

Table 3. Factors and Types of Development

Factor(s)	Type	Descriptors
Biology	Negative One-Sided	• Psychopathic • Paranoia • Criminal
Biology and Environment	Normal	• Adjustment • Little inner conflict • Fleeting maladjustment
	Positive One-Sided	• Prodigious achievement • High intellectual and imaginational • Low emotional overexcitability
Autonomous	Accelerated	• Strong overexcitability • Dynamisms • Positive disintegration • Transcendence of biology and environment

A note on Dąbrowski's use of accelerated development. Most of us who write about the theory of positive disintegration use *advanced development* to denote the process of general movement from lower to the highest forms of human functioning. That use of the phrase may leave the impression that development is linear and continuous, which would be inconsistent with the nature of the theory.

Dąbrowski (1996) describes a differentiated view of the process of development. Generally, it begins with sporadic experiences of disintegration, followed by re-integrations, referred to as *partial positive disintegrations,* because only discrete elements of lower functioning are destroyed and replaced by higher forms. Partial positive disintegrations, separated by periods of calm, represent advanced development because there is movement from lower to higher forms of functioning. When development progresses from episodic to continuous, Dąbrowski (1996) calls it *accelerated development.*

> ...the more development is advanced, i.e., the higher level it reaches, the less possible it is for it to slacken off and cease to carry on the process of psychic transformation. This is one reason why such advanced development was called accelerated (Dąbrowski, 1970). Here acceleration does not denote a rate of change toward completion but

> *rather the greatest extent and depth of the transformation of personality structure.* (p. 18)

In his discussion of deliberate nervous activity, Dąbrowski links it to the autonomous forces called dynamisms. The emergence of dynamisms is said to enhance the quality and extent of the highest form of nervous activity. In fact, it seems that dynamisms are part of this type of nervous activity: Dąbrowski states that dynamisms are higher forms of nervous system function.

Summary

Concepts of the theory of positive disintegration discussed in this chapter are limited to those that are relevant to understanding Dąbrowskian development, that is, movement from lower to higher levels of mental functioning. Multilevelness was Dąbrowski's great insight which differentiates his theory from other theories of development. That human development represents diverse forms that can be arranged in a hierarchy, ranging from lower, primitive functioning to higher, advanced functioning, is the philosophical basis of the theory. Developmental potential, a constitutional endowment, explains the multilevel forms of development by determining the level individuals can attain under ideal environmental circumstances. When there is sufficient developmental potential, that is, when all forms of overexcitability are inherited, advanced development can occur. The principle of positive disintegration and its mechanisms (dynamisms) explain how Dąbrowskian development occurs. Figure 7 is a representation of how developmental potential, positive disintegration and dynamisms create a particular level of development. The actual level is primarily influenced by the amount of developmental potential involved.

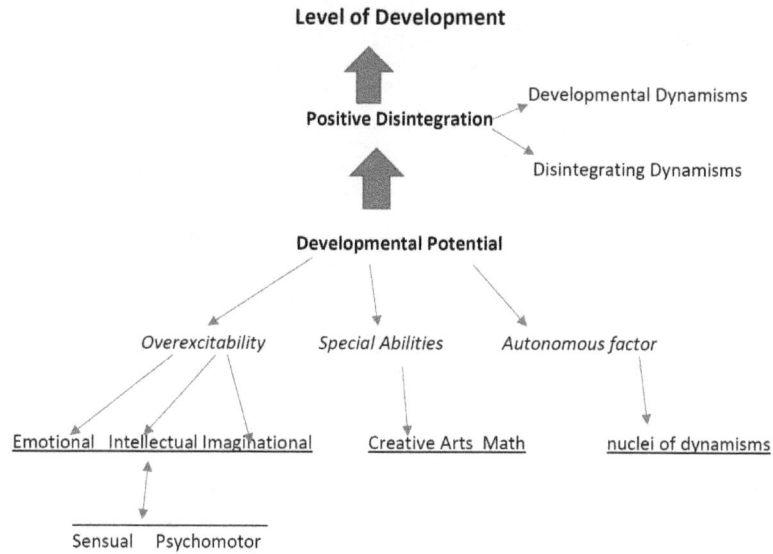

Note: The process of development is a function of Developmental potential, the presence of overexcitability. When all five forms are present, the lower forms, sensual and psychomotor, are transformed from their raw, primitive forms, by the higher forms to harness their energies for higher aims. Such developmental potential leads to positive disintegration composed of dynamisms. Overexcitability and the autonomous factor of developmental potential create the dynamisms enact positive disintegration. The level reached is determined by the amount of developmental potential.

Figure 7. Schematic Representation of Dąbrowskian Development

A final thought About the Selected Concepts. Dąbrowski's major constructs in the theory of positive disintegration are functionally entangled, creating a coherent whole. Positive disintegration, dynamisms and levels of development are not only interconnected, but they are also, in effect, synonyms for development. Any one of those three constructs is an answer to the question: What is development? Positive disintegration is development; dynamisms are development; progression through the levels is development. Developmental potential is an exception: it is essential for development, but it is not development itself.

CHAPTER 3
Key Psychological Constructs: A Dąbrowskian Perspective

Prior to my knowledge of the theory of positive disintegration, I had formulated my understanding of key constructs that were important for my counseling practice. These constructs included the following: childhood and socialization, self-concept, intelligence, and emotion. As my knowledge of Dąbrowski's theory deepened, the reframing of psychological constructs, characteristic of his theory, moved from the abstract realm to the concrete domain of my professional work. In this chapter, I discuss my original understanding of the constructs listed above and their reframing in the theory of positive disintegration.

Childhood and Socialization

As a great deal of my counseling practice involved parents of challenging children, it was important for me to have an understanding of the constructs of childhood and socialization. I begin by describing the conception of childhood followed by that of socialization prior to studying the theory of positive disintegration.

My conception of childhood includes two defining factors: *impulsivity* and *approval*. Impulsivity is an innate characteristic strongest in infants and young children. In my work with parents, I communicate my view of childhood impulsivity by the following statements: "I want what I want, when I want it. And that means now!" Children's behavior seems driven by moment-to-moment impulses, lacking conscious thought. This echoes Piaget's cognitive development theory, specifically the concept of egocentrism. Different from the idea of selfishness or narcissism, cognitive egocentrism refers to a child's experiencing of reality solely from their point of view. The notion of different points of view appears in later cognitive development. Piaget proclaimed that egocentric thought is not properly called *primitive*: it is normal cognition for young children. Analogously, impulsivity is not *pathological*, it is a normal childhood state. Both egocentrism and impulsivity are natural points of departure, which evolve and change over time.

I see a connection between Piaget's explanation of how egocentric thinking is transformed, and my understanding of how impulsivity is reduced. Egocentric thinking is changed not only by maturation but also by social interaction. Interactions with other children and adults who challenge children's cognitive expressions is an essential ingredient in the breakdown of cognitive egocentrism; maturation of thinking alone is not enough. Asking children to explain their statements, and the occurrence of disagreements with other children, are important ingredients in the reduction of egocentrism. Similarly, reduction of impulsivity is not accomplished by maturation alone. Increasing age will not suffice; social interaction is required. Children need feedback from the social environment to curb impulsivity. Socialization, meaning child rearing practices, teach children to inhibit naturally occurring impulses and conform to parents' demands. This is necessary for changing a child's behavior to delay the need for impulse gratification. Socialization commonly serves to teach compliance. Societal standards are inculcated in children by important people such as parents, family members and teachers. Without feedback from the social environment, impulsivity is not effectively reduced, regardless of age. Nonetheless, there is some transformation with age. For example, physical manifestations of impulsivity are internalized. The effects of unrestrained impulsivity in adolescence and adulthood ranges from lack of self-discipline and academic underachievement to unemployment and criminal behavior. Socialization is successful to the degree that it results in children learning to self-regulate and abide by societal norms and expectations.

Another important factor in childhood development is approval, and it is a byproduct of socialization. Parents and other caregivers raising young children communicate messages of approval and disapproval numerous times daily. Parents' values, both implicit and explicit, are manifested in feedback to children's behavior and by direct instruction. Inherent in these parental activities is the factor of approval. When children's behavior is consistent with parental standards, children receive approval, or, at least, avoid disapproval. It is a truism is that children want only approval from parents: approval feels good, disapproval feels bad. Regrettably for children, parents have the responsibility to engage in some form of socialization. There are some basic societal requirements for things such as toilet training, polite manners, appropriate expression of anger and frustration, and so forth, that parents need to fulfill. In other words, disapproval of some of children's naturally occurring behaviors is unavoidable in the socialization process. As a result, children learn to value parental approval—receiving approval feels good and they become dependent upon it. Similarly, parents feel good when they can communicate approval of children's behavior and they feel bad when they need to disapprove of their children's behaviors. Unfortunately for both parents and children, disapproval cannot be avoided because of the factor of impulsivity. Naturally occurring impulsivity requires socialization or it will have negative consequences for children.

Impulsivity also includes a time element. Children want what they want, and they want it immediately. I infer that children live moment-to-moment, in an ever-present 'now', so to speak. Living in a series of indistinguishable moments implies that children's behavior is motivated by impulses as they occur. As children begin to recognize the difference between approval and disapproval, the need for approval adds a motivational force for them. They want approval but are also ensnared by the force of impulsivity. I imagine that the child's experience is fluctuation between approval and impulsivity. With cognitive development as children get older, their sense of time evolves, and they can remember how they felt in past approvals and disapprovals. Their need for approval becomes conscious and contributes to the lessening of their impulsivity, the advent of self-regulation. Until the pendulum swings toward the need for approval, resulting in delay of gratification, impulsivity reigns. Before children begin to comply with parents' wishes, both children and parents will "feel bad", because the uncomfortable disapproval messages outweigh the preferable approval messages.

A final note about socialization. Unless individuals consciously attempt to replace learned attitudes, expectations and standards of behavior, the effects of socialization will be long lasting. Cognitive and behavioral habits which have developed in response to feedback from significant others, particularly parents, persist well into adulthood. New experiences with peers and other people may provide opportunities to rethink our established ways of living. However, as William James proclaimed long ago, habits are difficult to change.

The essences of *impulsivity*, which is inherent in our nature, and *approval*, which is a byproduct of socialization, receive significant treatment in the theory of positive disintegration. They appear as Dąbrowski's two forces of human development: biology and social environment. Though these factors are universally acknowledged, the difference in Dąbrowski's treatment of them is that, for advanced development to occur, the stranglehold of the two factors must be transcended. I think Dąbrowski would agree that a certain amount of impulsivity combined with a minimal amount of compliance with socialization are part of advanced development. Such 'controlled' impulsivity may give way to spontaneity and even creativity. A certain amount of conformity to societal standards, as taught through socialization, is in fact required to live in society.

Self-Concept

Self-concept has both descriptive and evaluative components. The descriptive part refers to factual matters such as physical characteristics, birth order, and cultural affiliations. The evaluative part, typically known as self-esteem, is the component of self-concept that exerts a great deal of influence on an individual's day to day life. Despite this distinction, self-concept and self-esteem are often used interchangeably. Self-esteem is a perennial concern of parents, teachers, and psychologists when they encounter signs of low self-esteem in their children, students, and clients, respectively. The goal is typically to create conditions for the development of high self-esteem/self-concept, given that the terms are often used synonymously.

Over the years, I have become concerned with low self-esteem, and have investigated ways of enhancing it. I began systematically by reviewing theories of self-concept development, and ultimately adopted a *reflected appraisals* approach, which has had a lasting influence on counseling clients. This approach proposes that self-concept and self-esteem arise and develop because of individuals' incorporating feedback received from significant others such as parents, family members and teachers. In short, self-concept is not present at birth; it arises from the socialization process. In effect, the daily feedback from caregivers during child rearing is grist for children's emerging cognition, which begins the creation of self-concept. Rudimentary concepts of 'self' become established in children as they comprehend and act upon the daily instructions provided by caregivers, particularly with the onset of language development. The socialization process communicates not only descriptive messages but also evaluative messages to children. Child-rearing requires communication of approval and disapproval; it is the internalization of these messages that children use to generate their sense of self-worth.

Although the goal of enhancing low self-esteem/self-concept and the reflected approach has served me well in counseling, they are a glaring contrast to the theory of positive disintegration. A mere perusal of the theory makes it clear that high self-esteem/self-concept is not a goal of development. In fact, periods of low self-esteem are *de facto* realities of the Dąbrowskian developmental process. The only self-descriptors that are consistent with the theory of positive disintegration are *self-knowledge* and *self-acceptance*. In addition, the reflected appraisals approach represents a powerful influence of the social environment, which is termed the second factor of development. Recall that for advanced development to occur, individuals need to transcend the influence of both the first factor (biology) and the second factor.

Intelligence

Intelligence, like other psychological constructs, is the subject of numerous theories with associated definitions. In my view, the lack of consensus on the nature of intelligence suggests that we do not really know what it is. One influence on my view of intelligence is Spearman's two factor theory that includes both general intelligence, and specific mental abilities. Application of Spearman's theory is seen in intelligence tests, such as the Wechsler tests. For example, the Wechsler Intelligence Scale for Children (5th Edition, WISC-V) defines intelligence as a combination of assessed general intelligence indicated by the full-scale score, and specific mental abilities as indicated by five distinct index scores (see 4).

Table 4. WISC-V: General Intelligence and Specific Mental Abilities

General Intelligence	Specific Mental Abilities
	Verbal comprehension
	Visual Spatial
Full Scale Intelligence Quotient	Fluid reasoning
	Working memory
	Processing Speed

Table 4 illustrates Spearman's theory that general intelligence is unitary; mental abilities are multiple expressions of general intelligence. When first developing his tests, Wechsler identified a set of mental abilities which he believed best defined intelligence. Intelligence is estimated by summing the adjusted scores on subtests, which measure those abilities. The index scores represent the main mental abilities assessed by the WISC-V. The FSIQ represents the level of general intelligence. I adopt this conception of intelligence in my view of general intelligence; and my concept of specific mental abilities differs from those visible in Wechsler's tests. For one thing, I do not equate intelligence with IQ. IQ is a good tool to assess accumulation of culturally bound learning, which is *related to* but not equal to intelligence *per se*. What I like to call "raw intelligence" represents *potential* to learn, to achieve, and so forth. Raw intelligence, as opposed to IQ (which is influenced by culture, social class, and opportunity) resides in brain physiology. As such, level of intelligence is a heritable quality which we currently cannot assess. Until research on brain physiology can measure *raw intelligence*, I must accept that Wechsler's tests are the best tools by which we can approximate intelligence levels.

Dąbrowski also espoused the notion of general intelligence, which is implied in his clinical work and specified in his research on gifted youth. In his comparative study of gifted and nongifted participants, he used the then-available edition of the Wechsler intelligence Scale for Children to differentiate the two groups. General intelligence is manifested by specific mental abilities, which are significantly more numerous than those included in the index scores of WISC-V. While I implicitly also consider a number of mental abilities in the course of my professional work with intellectually gifted clients, there are two that are of particular importance, namely, *awareness* and *analysis*. Clients who are identified as intellectually gifted commonly manifest greater than expected awareness, also called *heightened sensitivity*. In addition, they manifest great ability to analyze. They develop what I term an *analytic attitude*, referring to a tendency to spontaneously analyze everything and everyone they encounter.

Another approach to intelligence that has influenced my work is Piaget's theory. Piaget does not refer to a set of specific abilities that combine to form intelligence, but rather to a general process—adaptation. Intelligence is a function of assimilation and accommodation manifested in adaptation to the environment. When new information is encountered in the environment, physical or social, the new information is either assimilated into existing mental structures or accommodated by changing current mental structures. Novel stimuli and events disrupt the mental organization; assimilation or accommodation work to restore mental balance ('equilibration'). This perspective of intelligence led me to conclude that adaptation to the environment is beneficial; in fact, it is a sign of great intelligence. But the theory of positive disintegration, as I learned, takes a different stance on adaptation to the environment. It considers that adaptation or adjustment to the social environment, especially when it is mindless or automatic, is the antithesis of development.

Emotion

Emotion has been and continues to be the defining construct in my clinical work about human functioning. Motivated by the need to assist clients with their negative emotions, as well as to help myself, I felt compelled to create a conceptualization of emotion. My emphasis on emotion began with the counseling and psychotherapy approach by Carl Rogers. Rogerian therapy places exploration of client emotions front and center in the therapeutic process. Empathic responding to others' emotion, which is now ubiquitous, was one of Rogers' pioneering concepts. Though I learned how to respond effectively to emotions from Rogers, I had to learn about the concept of emotions from other sources. My conceptualization of emotion began with Piaget. His position was that cognition and emotion were different sides of the same coin. The interaction between cognition and emotion was made explicit to me first by reading Albert Ellis's discussions of rational emotive therapy, and later refined by the work of other authors, as well as reflection on my counseling practice. The basic proposition is that we create our emotions. Ellis made the little-known philosopher Epictetus famous in counseling and psychotherapy circles by attributing the following statement to him:It is not events that create emotions, it is our appraisal of events. This is the foundation of current therapies such as cognitive behavior therapy. Over time I developed a comprehensive theory of emotion to guide my clinical work. The rationale for the primacy of emotions in therapeutic endeavors was to create ways of helping clients reduce the negative emotions they brought to counseling, which led to more effective treatment of client concerns.

Though there is no explicit conceptualization of emotion evident in the theory of positive disintegration, it occupies a preeminent position. A major difference between my view of emotion and that of Dąbrowski's relates to negative emotions. In my original approach, all negative emotions need reduction; in Dąbrowski's approach, some negative emotions need celebration because they are indicators of advanced human development. The challenge posed by Dąbrowski's theory with respect to negative emotions is to determine which ones are in fact indicators of development.

Some Thoughts on Chapter 3

The effect of understanding the theory of positive disintegration on my key concepts has been most pronounced in my view of self-concept and emotions. The theory reinforced my established view that the goal of counseling should not be enhancement of self-concept but development of self-acceptance. Viewing self-concept as a social construction, in the theory of positive disintegration means that self-concept represents the influence of the social environment. As such, self-concept, especially its enhancement, is contradictory to the theory's view of advanced development. Transcending influences of the social environment is an important sign of the developmental process. Less concern with one's level of self-concept, then, is a sign of personal development.

Concern with clients' emotions has been an important part of counseling from the beginning of my professional practice. Naturally, the concern regarding emotions in counseling relates to clients' negative emotions. My view that a goal of counseling should be helping clients reduce negative emotions contradicted Dąbrowski's proclamation that negative emotions may signify the developmental process. Therefore, the goal of counseling is not to help clients reduce them but to help clients understand their negative emotions as positive signs. I was skeptical about this central proposition of the theory in my initial encounter of it. In time, I learned an important caveat regarding negative emotions. The proposition only applies to certain types of emotions: hose that emanate from individuals' experiencing of inner conflict.

CHAPTER 4
Feeling Bad Can be Good

The title of this chapter comes from one of the earliest conference sessions that I co-presented with Bill Tillier (Mendaglio & Tillier, 1993). I think it succinctly captures an essential proposition of the theory of positive disintegration. My task is to explain it.

Long before I encountered the theory of positive disintegration, I was drawn to understanding emotions. Some experiences in my youth made me aware of how passionately my family and I expressed emotions, both positive and negative. This is not surprising, considering that my family immigrated to Montreal from southern Italy, where I was born. There is some truth in stereotypes! I distinctly remember comments from my high school friends who had dinner at my home: "Sal, your family is emotion in motion!" This was the beginning of my appreciating the difference that culture makes in the expression of emotions. Later in life, this lesson was reinforced in a not so friendly way in other personal relationships with people of y Canadian culture. The essence of these experiences with Canadians went something like this: during discussion of a topic for which I felt a great deal of positive sentiment, and about which I spoke with enthusiasm and passion, I would hear the question: "Why are you angry?" I would say, "I am not angry." "But you sound angry." "I said I am NOT angry!" In time, I learned to curb the expression of my enthusiasm unless I was conversing with other Latin types, or at least, other people who were boisterous. And so, my interest in and concern with emotion began before my education as a psychologist, and well before I knew the name Kazimierz Dąbrowski.

Graduate preparation in psychology launched the development of my current thinking on emotions. Contributors to humanistic psychology, both the theory and the practice, emphasized the importance of emotions. Though these thinkers and practitioners, such as Carl Rogers, did not articulate a theory of emotions, they did emphasize the importance of a psychologist's empathic responses to a client's expression of feelings. In fact, encouraging a client's expressions of feelings is a fundamental tenet of the Rogerian approach to psychotherapy. Empathy, by which the therapist communicates nonjudgmental understanding and a compassionate attitude, leads to a deeper self-understanding by the client. Ultimately such learning led to my conclusion that, whether in therapy or daily life, a nonjudgmental attitude, one of acceptance, is essential for appropriate response to emotional expression occurring in therapeutic and personal relationships.

While acceptance of client emotions is useful in creating a good working relationship, the goal is the reduction, if not elimination, of a client's experience of negative emotions. Health professionals use various techniques to achieve that goal, such as relaxation training, meditation, and cognitive restructuring, and more recently, mindfulness. In effect, negative emotions are commonly viewed as symptoms to be remedied. My approach is different, but my goal is the same: help clients manage their negative emotions by teaching them my theory of emotions, and by helping them accept their emotions. Thus, many health professionals and I see different means to the same end: reduce negative emotions.

In my early studies of Dąbrowski's theory, when my understanding of it was quite superficial, I noticed that I had in common with him a belief in the importance of emotion. I soon began to realize that he, too, was very interested in negative emotions. But the initial similarity that I had perceived vanished as I learned the goals of our mutual interest were radically different. While I viewed all negative emotions as problematic, he was adamant that some negative emotions were to be celebrated, not accepted in order that they can be reduced, and not eliminated. According to Dąbrowski, the experience of negative emotions by *some* individuals is a sign of personal growth requiring nurturing, not a symptom requiring psychological intervention. While learning Dąbrowski's perspective on negative emotions, questions arose in my mind: *What types of emotions are involved? How can negative emotions create growth? Who are the individuals in whom negative emotions may be signs of growth?* With a better grasp of the theory of positive development, I can propose answers.

What types of negative emotions indicate growth?

We are interested in negative emotions produced by a particular type of conflict. Conflict results from cognitive awareness of at least two incongruent thoughts, choices, or courses of action. In this sense, conflict itself is not an emotion but rather a cognitive *process* that creates negative emotions. In the theory of positive disintegration, it is the negative emotions produced by *inner conflict* that are considered signs of Dabrowskian development. For Dąbrowski, inner conflict is the experience of discrepancy between "what is" and "what ought to be". This formulation of inner conflict applies to external and internal events. Awareness of discrepancy between the way the world is (e.g., nations at war) and the way it should be (e.g., nations cooperating) has the power of producing sadness, disappointment, anger, and frustration. Awareness of the discrepancy in external events may cause conflict within self, such as "I should be doing something to help those in need, but I am not." In the theory of positive disintegration, this is known as multilevel conflict, a 'vertical' assessment of discrepancy between higher and lower levels of morality. Through the process of self-evaluation, using the criterion of "what I ought to be", awareness of shortcomings becomes evident. Realization that behaviors are morally lower than they should be produces intense, persistent negative emotions, such as shame, guilt, anxiety, with the potential of leading to existential depression. Emotions generated through multilevel inner conflict should be fostered because they create growth.

How can negative emotions create growth?

Growth or development in the theory of positive disintegration is a progression from lower to higher ways of being. Positive disintegration is the process and dynamisms are its instruments. The negative emotions emanating from multilevel conflict are manifestations of disintegrating dynamisms: one feels shame, guilt, astonishment, disquietude, inferiority, and dissatisfaction. These dynamisms operating alone or in combination, work to destroy lower forms of daily functioning, sometimes rapidly, sometimes gradually. While the destructive dynamisms operate in a nuanced manner, it is possible to distill a common mental procedure that includes awareness, standards, and evaluation, creating multilevel conflict, which yields emotions. For the process to occur there needs to be awareness of behavior or thinking, and some standard to which it is compared. When behavior, for example, does not meet the standard, conflict ensues and various negative emotions such as disappointment or anxiety are generated. Initially the standards are the product of socialization, and their breach creates shame. In time, standards are replaced by a set of values that are internal in nature. Breaching of values adopted by individuals creates guilt and depression. Experience of chronic emotional pain that can be rather intense provides motivation for the resolution of specific instances of multilevel conflict. When a certain threshold of pain is reached, varying with each person, a crossroads emerges, the choice of adopting the higher value-laden form, or continuing with the current lower-level form. Development is enhanced when the conflict is resolved by commitment to the higher form. Negative emotions—dynamisms of disintegration—serve the growth process when they encourage the selection of higher functioning to resolve the suffering of the multilevel conflict.

Autonomy describes a form of development in which the predominant motivation is to live one's values: a system of positive values is created which controls biological urges. Autonomy, personal responsibility, altruism, and empathy characterize this type of development. While biological development is automatic (in that we do not have to create the instincts of self-preservation and hunger drive), autonomous development (breaking the bonds of biology) is achieved by individual choice. Feeling bad is not only an essential precursor, but also a requirement, for the process leading to autonomous development. This leads to the third question: Who are the people whose negative emotions can propel them onto the path of development?

Who are the individuals for whom negative emotions may be signs of growth?

The people in question are found in every racial, cultural, ethnic, economic, and age group. There is only one feature that differentiates such people from others in their groups: developmental potential. According to the theory, some people inherit varying degrees of developmental potential. As described in Chapter 2, developmental potential consists of overexcitability, special abilities and talents, and the third factor (autonomous forces, or dynamisms). Overexcitability is the major component by which developmental potential is assessed.

To review, overexcitability has five forms: sensual, psychomotor, imaginational, intellectual, and emotional. Not all forms are of equal value: sensual and psychomotor are lower forms; imaginational, intellectual, and emotional are higher forms. The individuals in question possess psychomotor and sensual overexcitability, but they also have one or more of the higher forms; some people possess all five forms. Regardless of the combination, emotional overexcitability is an essential part of the constellation of forms required for development to occur. In addition, some individuals may have special abilities and talents (e.g., musical, or mathematical). The seed of the third factor, i.e., the impetus for autonomy, is also evident. The presence of higher forms of overexcitability is the basic requirement for production of the type of negative emotions that should be nurtured. Though the theory does not explicitly include intelligence in the notion of developmental potential, level of intelligence is understood in overexcitability and other aspects of the theory. High level of intelligence is implicit in the description of intellectual form, which includes love of learning, curiosity, asking probing questions and so forth. Having said this, Dąbrowski is quick to add that intellectual overexcitability and intelligence are not synonyms, implying that high intelligence can occur without intellectual overexcitability. In general, the individuals in question have some or all the higher forms of overexcitability and a well above average level of intelligence.

A consequence of overexcitability is significantly enhanced experience of external and internal stimuli. That is, overexcitability makes individuals highly sensitive to stimuli and leads to an intensification of response to them. In practice this means individuals are very sensitive, very aware of the world around them, of other people, and of themselves. Responses to external and internal events are intensified. Magnification of responses is particularly evident in situations eliciting emotions. Whether it is a sense of awe in response to a piece of music, or feeling distraught at the plight of others, the experience is greater than one would expect. It is important to note that not all such emotional experiences are shared intentionally with others; expression of intense feelings may simply occur due to their intensity—they are so strong that they simply burst out. Alternately, the emotions may be shared with a trusted individual, or simply experienced in solitude. It is *experiencing* that overexcitability creates; it does not include *expression*, which is influenced by other factors (e.g., culture).

The idea that only some people are characterized by developmental potential, specifically by overexcitability, may elicit some resistance. I view this part of the theory in the context of individual differences of heritable traits, which is well established in various fields of study, including psychology. Further, I see elements of overexcitability in the currently used phrase, *wired differently*, an informal yet effective way of describing these individuals. Being *wired differently* may refer to people who are exceptional, odd, or weird, though these descriptors are usually positive in tone. The concept of being wired differently is also found in scholarly works, in which *wiring* refers to the central nervous system. There is some support for the idea that the brains of creative individuals are different from normal people. I think that Dąbrowski would be comfortable using the term *wired differently* as a shorthand reference to developmental potential. Recall that his definition of overexcitability refers the central nervous system, easily understood to be one that is wired differently.

Feeling bad can be good, when the source of bad feelings is inner conflict.

PART II:
Dąbrowskian Development

Chapter 5 Levels of Development
Chapter 6 Emergence of Disintegrating Dynamisms
Chapter 7 Emergence of Developmental Dynamisms

Chapter 5
Levels of Development

Dąbrowski explains how personality—the pinnacle of development—is achieved through five levels of positive disintegration. To appreciate the structure of the five levels, I will elucidate some of the concepts underlying Dąbrowskian development. Developmental potential is worth reviewing because of its pivotal role in development. There are two other concepts related to development: the use of *level* as opposed to *stage* of development; and *rate* of development. Description of the five levels of development follows a discussion of the three concepts.

Developmental Potential

Development, in the theory of positive disintegration, is largely determined by developmental potential, which is a heritable characteristic. The social environment is implicated, but it is the degree of potential that ultimately sets a ceiling on development. The theory does not provide a measure by which we can easily quantify this inherited characteristic. However, there are some guidelines. Developmental potential is effectuated by interaction with the social environment. Social environmental influence is apparent when a moderate amount of the potential is inherited. A supportive environment will facilitate actualization of potential, whereas a non-supportive social environment will interfere with it. When potential is very low or very high, the quality of the social environment is not a factor. With very low potential there is no development, even with the most supportive social environment; with very high potential, there *is* development, even with the least supportive social environment. In terms of assessing the amount of developmental potential, measuring overexcitability is the proposed method. Developmental potential is strongest when all five forms of overexcitability are present. Presumably, a lack of overexcitability, or the presence of only one or two of the lower forms (sensual, psychomotor), has a negative influence on development. Progression through the levels of development, then, assumes the inheritance of all forms of overexcitability.

Levels Not Stages

Dąbrowski (1996) differentiates level of development from stage of development. Level refers to a collection of developmental factors that create an identifiable mental organization. Developmental factors for each level are defined as a set of dynamisms unique to that level. Unlike stage, there is no age, nor any time frame associated with level. In stage theories of development, higher stage is *built upon the previous stage*, leading to the notion of transition from one stage up to another. Such transition does not apply to the theory of positive disintegration because a higher level *replaces* a lower level. Attainment or achievement of a level means that the mental organization of the lower level is destroyed and replaced by the organization of the new level. One last quality that distinguishes level from stage is that more than one level can exist simultaneously, while in stage theories only one stage at a time exists. When more than two or more levels exist, conflict is inevitable and is resolved when one level predominates.

Rate of Development

Another concept regards the rate of development—it does not occur at an even pace. There are times when the factors of development—the dynamisms of a level—are particularly active at creating experiences of anxiety and depression, which are followed by a psychological equilibrium. During such plateaus of development, dynamisms continue to use newly acquired higher mental structures to guide behavior, but they do not create further transformation. Development may stop at such plateaus because of limited developmental potential. In such cases, the result is partial positive integration, with no possibility of achieving the highest levels. When development proceeds beyond plateaus due to great intensity of developmental potential, it is unlikely that development will diminish and cease to produce greater psychic transformation. In essence, the higher the level of development, the more difficult it is to stop development.

Five Levels of Development

Dąbrowskian development is defined by five clearly distinguishable levels: primary integration, unilevel disintegration, spontaneous multilevel disintegration, organized multilevel disintegration and secondary integration. The three levels of disintegration transform the primitive functioning of primary integration into the exemplary human functioning of secondary integration. My summary of the five levels of development is an interpretation of Dąbrowski (1970, pp. 21-24; 1996, pp. 18-20), thereby providing readers with the general "flavor" of each level. It is difficult to discuss levels of development without considering dynamisms, because they are the mechanisms of positive disintegration. The five levels with key descriptors and associated dynamisms are summarized in Table 5. In the following discussion, I will outline the dynamics of each level.

Table 5. Five Levels of Development: Key Descriptors and Dynamisms

Level of Development	Main Descriptors	Main Dynamisms
V. Secondary Integration	• Achievement of personality • What ought to be is • Compassion • Self-sacrifice • Exemplar of humanity • Rare achievement	• Personality ideal • Responsibility • Autonomy • Authentism
IV. Organized Multilevel Disintegration	• Resolution of inner conflict • Systemization of thinking • Self-direction of development • Third (autonomous) factor in control • Values direct behaviort	• Subject-object in oneself • Empathy • Third factor • Inner psychic transformation • Self-awareness • Self-control • Education of one self • Autopsychotherapy

Level		
III. Spontaneous Multilevel Disintegration	• Multilevel Inner conflict • Hierarchization active • "What is" vs "What ought to be" • Real vs Ideal self • Negative self evaluation • Behavior-standards discrepancy • Socialized standards to creation of values • Destruction of lower functioning • Crucial level for advanced development	• Hierarchization • Positive Maladjustment "Self" Dynamisms: • Shame • Astonishment • Guilt • Inferiority Disquietude • Dissatisfaction
II. Unilevel Disintegration	• Loosening of rigid mental structure • Triggered by maturation and environmental events • Doubt, indecision • Circular thinking • Horizontal conflict • Nuclei of hierarchization	• Ambivalence • Ambitendencies
I. Primary Integration	• Rigid mental structure • Little or no reflection • Adevelopment **Subtypes** Normal: • Controlled by First and Second Factors Psychopathic: • Controlled by First Factor	No dynamisms

Level I: Primary Integration

Primary integration is characterized by mental structures and behaviors that are of low level. Dąbrowski occasionally refers to Level I as *primitive*, which seems more appropriate because it enables us to conjure up the nascent, autonomic aspects of this level. Cognitive processing is automatic and impulsive, a product of a rigid mental organization which helps satisfy instinctual, primitive drives. Drive satisfaction may be achieved in ways consistent with societal prescriptions, or by disregarding them. Any conflict that is produced in the process is, by and large, oriented externally; little inner conflict is apparent at this level. In fact, there is minimal, if any, self-reflection or questioning of societal expectation. This is not surprising, since regardless of level, the use of intelligence is largely concerned with addressing drives and needs, and, therefore, unavailable for much reflection.

Dąbrowski subdivides primary integration into two subtypes of development, *normal* and *psychopathic*, depending on which factors are in control, as seen in Figure 8.

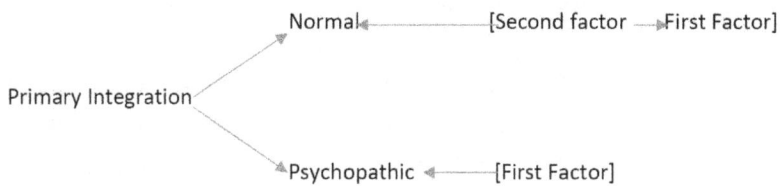

Note: Two subtypes of primary integration are controlled by respective factors of development. The difference between normal primary integration and psychopathic primary integration is that, in the normal subtype, the second factor tames the first factor. Without the influence of the second factor, primary integration would simply be psychopathic development.

Figure 8. Subtypes of Primary Integration and Controlling Factors of Development

While normal development is controlled by both the first and second factors (biology and environment), psychopathic development is controlled by the first factor exclusively. In normal primary integration, satisfaction of innate drives is attenuated by the influence of the social environment. With the influence of this second factor, innate drives are satisfied by societally sanctioned ways. The influence of this second factor, active through socialization practices, is manifested in the need to comply with societal standards, thereby avoiding punishment and disapproval. To accomplish this combination of goals, individuals automatically comply with societal standards is learned.

One way to capture aspects of my depiction of normal primary integration is to equate it with Socrates' "unexamined life". In psychopathic primary integration, not only is life unexamined, but life is also predatory. Patterns of thinking are in the service of egocentric drive satisfaction. Socially appropriate behavior, including expressions of altruism and empathy, is a scam, a tool to satisfy impulsive aims. Normal and psychopathic developments do occur in their absolute forms. There are occurrences of normal behavior in which individuals conform without exception to societal prescriptions. Regrettably there are occurrences of psychopathic behavior in which individuals are driven completely by biological drives. However, normal individuals occasionally may use other people for their own ends; and psychopathic individuals may from time to time behave normally. In other words, normal and psychopathic are not absolute categories, but both demonstrate primary integration.

Thoughts on Rigid Mental Organization of Primary Integration. In describing primary integration, I use words that are similar, if not identical to the ones Dąbrowski uses; for example, "rigid mental organization" and "little or no self-reflection". Rigid mental organization consists of habits and task-focused mental activity, combined with lack of reflection. A defining characteristic of habit is unconsciousness or automaticity; as Dąbrowski might say, behaviors occur with limited or complete lack of awareness. Furthermore, habit is often associated with an undesirable pattern of behavior that we wish to change. However, as William James pointed out over a century ago, habits are not solely negative; many habits make our daily lives easier. Positive habits include activities that we take for granted, to which we give little or no thought. Consider tying shoelaces, enacting a morning routine, or walking, for that matter. We tie our shoelaces without thinking; we do our morning routine without actually thinking about each part; and we walk, without being aware of each step we take. Once learned, we are rarely conscious of these activities as we perform them until changes occur: putting on a pair of new hiking boots, beginning the morning on a vacation in a hotel room, or walking on rough terrain. Novel situations spark thinking about activities that normally do not require conscious evaluation. And so it goes with acts of thinking in daily life: when not engaged in habitual behavior, we engage in *task-focused thinking*, which refers to mental activity directly related to tasks that we *choose* to perform in daily life, given our developmental stage. A defining characteristic of this type of thinking is a primarily external focus. Children and adolescents engage in task-focused thinking when dealing with school matters, attending to parental and educational prescriptions, and during play. Similarly, adults demonstrate task-focused thinking while dealing with work duties, raising children, and daily household matters.

Habitual behavior and task-focused thinking are products of socialization and are characteristic of development controlled by the second factor (social environment). Implicit in this form of development is the influence of the first factor—biology. Rigid mental organization refers to patterns of thinking—mental habits—developed to satisfy biological drives in ways sanctioned by society. Rigid mental organization describes well-worn pathways in the brain produced largely by the influence of the social environment. Socialization not only controls *behavior*, it also controls how and *what we think*. With its emphasis on conformity, society does not generally encourage reflective thought. We are not encouraged to ask "why"; we are expected to conform to society's dictates. Mental activity is generally directed externally, aimed at learning and enacting behaviors and attitudes that are consistent with societal prescriptions. Habits and task-focused thinking associated with daily living create a mental organization that is solidified by the superordinate learning needed to comply with societal norms and values. Internally directed thinking (reflection) appears when behavior and attitudes are inconsistent with societal expectations. Self-reflection with the aim of personal growth appears sporadically. It is the relative unquestioning compliance and general lack of self-reflection (a lack of consciousness) that make the mental organization of primary integration rigid.

Primary integration is an essential component of the theory of positive disintegration because the foundation of the theory is multi-levelness. Dąbrowski observed that the variety of human development can be arranged from lower to higher, with different gradations in between the two extremes. Primary integration describes the lowest form of development, but is it development? To be consistent with the theory of positive disintegration, I think that the term *adevelopmental* (i.e., without development, a word also used by Dąbrowski) is a better descriptor for this Level. Neither normal nor psychopathic primary integration can be thought of as development; it is better to call it *adevelopment*. I wonder whether Level I (primary integration) should be included in "levels of development." For any other theory, this would not be an issue, but Dąbrowski's theory is unique. His definition of development does *not* include primary integration: there is no movement, no progression to the next level. Dąbrowskian development does not begin until Level II.

Level II: Unilevel Disintegration

Loosening of the rigid mental structure of primary integration signals the onset of unilevel disintegration. Disintegration at Level II is rudimentary, but sufficient to create a slackening of rigid mental organization, which consists of habits, task-focused thinking, and little reflection. Specific changes include increased awareness of bodily sensations, circularity of thinking, mood fluctuations, anxiety, depression, and indecision. It becomes difficult to decide upon and commit to courses of action. These are the superficial beginnings of inner conflict (a hallmark of the process of development for Dąbrowski) relating to choices of equal moral values. At this level, conflict consists of consideration of choices that are on the same level morally speaking. Hence the name unilevel disintegration for Level II. The two dynamisms, called ambivalence and ambitendencies, are unique to this level, and are responsible for disrupting the original, rigid mental organization. Ambivalence refers to experiencing of incompatible feelings, such as like and dislike, approach and avoidance, love and hate. Ambitendencies refers to experiencing inability to decide among courses of action, and simultaneous desire for two incompatible goals, resulting in self-defeating behavior.

Assuming that an increase in self-reflection is responsible for the loosening of the rigid mental organization of primary integration, the question becomes, "what triggers the reflective process?" By its descriptor "rigid", the mental organization is viewed as so ingrained that an event of major proportions is necessary to start the unravelling of mental structures and spark new mental processing. The reflective process begins with certain types of biological and environmental events. Puberty is a maturational milestone that has the power to begin an attack on the grip of primary integration. Regardless of any Dąbrowskian interpretation, puberty is disruptive of the status quo for all adolescents. Adolescence has been long acknowledged as a tumultuous time characterized by the phrase "the storm and stress" of adolescence. Physical changes, incipient sexuality, and psychological issues such as identity and need for belonging, wreak havoc on pre-pubescent patterns of thinking and behaving. While puberty is an age-related event that is mentally disruptive, natural and social environmental events have similar power. Catastrophic events of nature such as wildfires, hurricanes, floods, and earthquakes are disruptive of both physical and mental structures. Environmental crises, beyond triggering the self-preservation instinct, also spark increases in self-reflection. Death of loved ones or others in one's social circle, especially when untimely and unexpected, can initiate mental disintegration.

The disintegration is termed *unilevel* because the elements of mental processing of Level II—desires, attitudes, standards, and behavior—are not conceived of hierarchically. Specifically, conflicts that develop are of a *horizontal* rather than of a vertical nature. Horizontal conflicts manifest ambivalence between choices undifferentiated, morally speaking. In contrast, multilevel conflict is deemed *vertical* because the struggle to decide is between choices that are perceived as morally lower or higher. Multilevel conflict requires that the dynamism of hierarchization is fully activated.

Maturational and environmental events serve to loosen rigid mental organization, the effect of which may be temporary or long-lasting. Developmental potential determines the longevity of disruption. Insufficient potential results in only temporary disruptions of established patterns of thinking, with a return to primary integration. A sufficiency of developmental potential results in lasting effects. Strong developmental potential consists of the presence of the five forms of overexcitability, from which dynamisms emerge. Dynamisms, as I indicated in Chapter 2, are the mechanisms of positive disintegration. Level II marks the first appearance of dynamisms, *namely*, *ambivalence* and *ambitendency*, which are responsible for disrupting rigid mental organization as described earlier in this chapter.

Thoughts on Level II Unilevel Disintegration. Level II is a transition phase from the adevelopmental level of primary integration to the onset of Dąbrowskian development. Though Dąbrowski identifies puberty as a likely trigger of this level—assuming sufficient developmental potential—he does not equate levels of development with age. The implication is that individuals may experience the disruption of puberty but return to primary integration, only to experience developmental disruption at a later age. Further, while this level is conceived of as a temporary state, Dąbrowski does not specify its duration: does it last for three weeks or three months or a year? We can surmise that the longer it lasts, the more psychologically dangerous it is because the uncertainty and doubt that it creates may lead to serious mental illness and suicide. However, with sufficient developmental potential, individuals at this level begin to demonstrate the seeds of the dynamisms of Level III. Such individuals may soon long for the old days of primary integration as they are propelled into the beginnings of the turbulence of Level III.

Level III Spontaneous Multilevel Disintegration

The distinguishing characteristic of Level III is the beginning of inner conflict. The external conflicts of primary integration, as well as the horizontal conflicts of unilevel disintegration are gradually replaced by multilevel inner conflict. In the theory of positive disintegration, multilevel inner conflict is defined as increasing awareness of the discrepancy between "what is" and "what ought to be", between the real and the ideal. Awareness of discrepancies causing inner conflict applies to both external social phenomena and to oneself. At the global level, perceived discrepancies include seeing how leaders who should be caring for their people are in fact mistreating them. At the local level, perceived discrepancies include observing how authorities in the workplace use their power for self-aggrandizement rather than supporting employees. When applied to self, perception of discrepancy refers to awareness of inconsistency between 'the way I ought to be' and 'the way I am', between the ideal and real selves. This multilevel perception of reality creates inner conflict that causes negative emotions which can be of intense magnitude, such as existential anxiety and clinical depression.

Underlying the experience of inner conflict is the dynamism of hierarchization, which organizes mental phenomena and behavioral events from lower to higher in moral value. The workings of the dynamism of hierarchization are seen in a series of what I call "self" dynamisms, because the theme of self-evaluation pervades them. Their function is to destroy lower forms of thinking, feeling and behavior, associated with "what is" in one's self. The "self" dynamisms are negative emotions produced by negative self-evaluations: feelings of shame, guilt, inferiority, internal disquietude, and personal dissatisfaction. *Shame* is distress emanating from self-consciousness and embarrassment in response to perceived or real unexpected negative response from the social environment. Because of its external social environmental connection, shame may begin in Level II and is among the first disintegrating dynamisms to appear. Along with feelings of shame, *astonishment with oneself* is a dynamism that emerges early in Level III. Astonishment is the feeling produced by a growing awareness of self and others. Increased awareness of one's thoughts, emotions, and behaviors leads to bewilderment and unpleasant surprises. Similarly, with growing awareness of other people's behaviors, there is a mixture of both amazement and shock. *Guilt* is a dynamism that occurs in the context of relationships. Negative feelings arise when one's attitude or behavior toward another is contrary to standards of behavior. Initially the standards against which individuals compare their thoughts and actions are those internalized by the socialization process. These standards are in due course replaced by a set of values created by individuals themselves: socialized values that are seen as higher are kept, while those perceived as lower are rejected. *Feelings of inferiority in oneself* are different from the common usage of *inferiority*, which is the result of social comparison. The *dynamism* of inferiority is an internal comparison of the ideal aspirational level with the actual level of development. Inferiority feelings arise out the perception of personal inadequacy with respect to one's values. Being unfaithful to one's values produces shock; this strong emotional response ultimately has the effect of instigating more effort to adhere to one's growing commitment to a set of positive values. Feeling inferior in oneself sparks another related dynamism, *disquietude*. Disquietude creates internal discomfort when ongoing impulsivity, lack of self-control, and other forms of primitive behaviors continue unabated. While inferiority in oneself is considered a strong dynamism promoting disintegration, *dissatisfaction with oneself* is considered the most powerful of Level III dynamisms. It consists of persistent frustration and unhappiness with one's self because evaluation of behavior, including behavior with other people, is inconsistent with one's aspirational values. Thus, dissatisfaction becomes a strong indicator of the potential for advanced development.

In addition to the 'self' dynamisms, Level III dynamisms include *positive maladjustment.* This relates to an individuals' maladjustment to, or active rejection of, socialized mores and expectations, and their effort to replace these with adjustment to and conformity with their aspirational values. Positive maladjustment has its origins in Level III and comes to full fruition in Level IV.

Level III is crucial for advanced development: spontaneous multilevel disintegration significantly magnifies the loosening of the rigid mental organization that began in unilevel disintegration. The dawn of awareness, specifically, awareness of self and other as well as the budding hierarchization of Level II, reach maturity in Level III. Increased awareness underpins new mental processes. For example, circularity of thinking is replaced by more thoughtful consideration of issues; awareness of self leads to self-evaluation; awareness of others leads to an appreciation of their uniqueness; and hierarchization leads to multilevel perception of reality. With continual awareness of the discrepancy between what is and what ought to be—multilevel inner conflict, and the ensuing experiencing of intense negative emotions, rigid mental organization is eroded and eventually transformed into a more flexible, advanced and morally higher mental pattern.

Spontaneous multilevel disintegration is a level of development fraught with experiences of intense negative emotions such as anxiety, guilt, frustration, and shame brought on primarily by negative self-evaluation. The root cause is persistent awareness of numerous examples of discrepancy between the real and the ideal self. Self-evaluation is not possible without a set of standards against which to compare oneself. It is the discrepancy between behavior or thinking on the one hand, and standards on the other, that creates inner conflict. At the beginning of Level III, the standards and values used for comparison purposes are learned through child-rearing practices and societal institutions. As hierarchization progresses, socialized standards and values themselves become subjected to scrutiny from the point of view of higher and lower: standards deemed lower are rejected; those deemed higher are accepted. One of the important outcomes of Level III is an individual's conscious creation of a set of values by which they aspire to live. The personal set of values is then used for self-evaluation purposes.

Self-evaluation is the key factor causing development in Level III, and this is supported by the recognition that the dynamisms responsible for transformation in this level occur within the self: astonishment with oneself, feelings of shame, guilt and inferiority in oneself, disquietude and dissatisfaction with oneself. Dynamisms of Level III are discussed in detail in Chapter 6.

Thoughts on Level III Spontaneous Multilevel Disintegration. *Spontaneous* means that disintegrative processes are unplanned and unstructured: dynamisms occur in response to environmental events and internal stimuli. For example, feelings of shame are responses to awareness of self in relation to the social environment; inferiority toward oneself may result from becoming conscious that behavior in a social situation may have been inconsistent with one's aspirational values. As such, dynamisms may arise unexpectedly, especially in the early phases of Level III, dynamisms not yet under control by the individual. The use of 'multilevel' to describe Level III denotes that individuals begin to differentiate phenomena as higher and lower, particularly with reference to morality. *Multilevelness* of experience is an important achievement of this level, differentiating it from Level II, which involves *unilevel* disintegration.

Level IV Organized Multilevel Disintegration

Whereas inner conflict is the hallmark of Level III, resolution is the distinguishing feature of Level IV. Systemization of thinking, behavior and tranquility replace the mental chaos and emotional turmoil of Level III; directed development replaces the spontaneous disintegration of lower functioning. No longer reactive to internal and external stimuli, individuals take charge of their own development, which is now controlled by the third factor (autonomy) rather than the first and second factors (biology and environment). The set of values which was in its infancy amid the conflicts of Level III is clearly elaborated; positive values influence thinking and motivate behavior. With the achievement of Level IV, the inner conflict of Level III is replaced by a principled response to external conflict arising from situations which are inconsistent with one's set of values. One's values are no longer simply aspirational; they are lived day to day. An important development in Level IV is an individual's clearer and more distinct image of their personality ideal—the person they aspire to be. Empathy predominates, creating positive attitudes towards other people, thereby motivating altruistic behavior.

Unlike the dynamisms of Level III that function to destroy primitive ways of thinking and being, the dynamisms of Level IV represent advances in development. The names of the dynamisms themselves indicate their qualitative difference when compared to dynamisms of previous Levels: self-awareness and self-control, subject and object in oneself syntony, identification and empathy, the third factor inner psychic transformation, education of oneself, and autopsychotherapy. Description of each dynamism follows. *Self-awareness* and *self-control* include awareness of one's mental and behavioral activities, personal identity and uniqueness, and the realization that some personality traits are more important than others. Awareness enables individuals to engage in self-control. *Subject and object in oneself* refers to the process of self-observation and self-examination for the purpose of furthering one's mental development. Through active, constant self-exploration, individuals comprehend the essential elements of their inner life. Through this dynamism an individual ultimately comes to experience his or her own essence—what he or she truly is. Syntony, identification, and empathy are progressively more complex modes of relating to other individuals.

Syntony is an automatic process of feeling what others feel, a sympathetic response to other people's emotions; it is analogous to emotional contagion. *Identification* is more cognitive and somewhat more conscious than syntony and refers to understanding others. *Empathy* refers to gaining insight into others' experiences, and including their emotions, combined with an altruistic attitude toward others.

The *third factor* is the agent of conscious choice in development, seen as the inner self that co-ordinates an individual's mental life. This dynamism discriminates among functions and events according to their value for enhancing development: if they are not growth promoting, they are rejected. *Inner psychic transformation* is the process by which instincts and drives are sublimated into positive moral values. These values are gradually incorporated into one's personality ideal. Thus, primitive impulses are not only consciously rejected but are also transformed. *Education of oneself* and *autopsychotherapy* function to actualize personal ideals by engaging in self-improvement, guided by an individual's hierarchy of values. Autopsychotherapy is the process of educating and guiding oneself during experiences of stress: the ability to cope with distress whether it originates in external or internal environments. For Dąbrowski, individuals who reach the higher levels of functioning literally become their own teachers and psychotherapists.

Level V Secondary Integration

The hallmark of Level V, the highest level of Dąbrowskian development, is the achievement of personality, the epitome of human development. With the attainment of Level IV and Level V, the process of positive disintegration is complete and is no longer active. Secondary integration is rarely achieved and is manifested only in genuine exemplars of humanity who live their lives guided by their set of positive values, manifested in their compassion and self-sacrifice. At this Level, "what ought to be" becomes "what is". Growth continues, though it is driven not by disintegration but rather by self-perfection—motivation to become fully human, pursuing causes aimed at the betterment of humankind.

The dynamisms of secondary integration are: responsibility for self and others, autonomy, authentism, and personality ideal. *Responsibility for oneself and for others* refers to taking responsibility for one's own actions, thinking and desires, in the context of one's life and in relationships with others. Other people are not seen as objects; individuals develop an I-thou relationship with other people. A sense of responsibility, that is, the need to take ownership of one's shortcomings and repair them, extends to helping others who wish to improve. *Autonomy* is the dynamism by which individuals consciously free themselves from lower drives, and from aspects of the social environment that contradict positive values. *Authentism*, based on self-awareness, is the expression of one's emotions, cognitions, and attitudes. It refers to being consistent with one's hierarchy of values. *Personality ideal* is a standard against which an individual evaluates her or his actual personality. It eventually becomes the highest dynamism that shapes one's personality.

Suggestions Regarding the Five Levels of Development

After much reflection on the Levels, some possible refinement came to mind. These include: primary integration as adevelopmental, progression through Levels not stages, and renaming Level IV.

Primary integration: adevelopment, not level of development. When I consider the level of primary integration in the context of development in the theory of positive disintegration, I conclude that it should not be included in levels of development. I have proposed that "adevelopmental", a word that Dąbrowski himself uses to denote the absence of development, is a more appropriate designation for Level I. What is currently described as primary integration corresponds with a traditional concept of normal development, not the Dąbrowskian concept. In fact, Dąbrowski himself refers to individuals at Level I as "so-called normal". Primary integration, then, would refer to the traditional development that is the product of physical maturation from infancy to later adulthood and socialization, including child rearing practices and acculturation by societal institutions. For those with sufficient developmental potential, primary integration would be a springboard for Dąbrowskian development. For others not so endowed, normality continues throughout life.

As I noted earlier and repeated in Figure 8 (see p. XX), I subdivided primary integration into normal and psychopathic. With this reconfiguration of levels of development, I suggest that only *normal* primary integration, controlled by first and second factors, combined with developmental potential can lead to unilevel disintegration (see Figure 9). I cannot envision the psychopathic subtype, controlled solely by the first factor, being a precursor of development. *Psychopathic* primary integration leads to negative development (e.g., criminality). Removing primary integration from the Levels of development would leave four Levels.

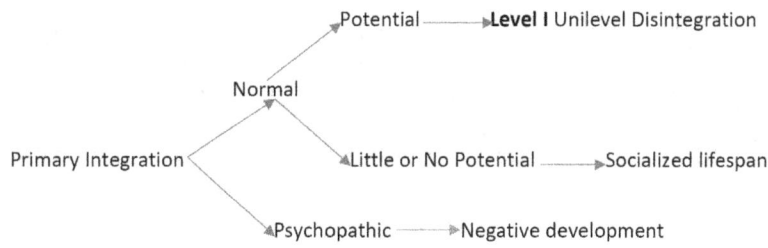

Figure 9. Primary Integration and its Relationship to Levels of Development

Progression through Levels not stages. It is noteworthy to recall that developmental potential sets a ceiling on development. Depending on the amount of the potential inherited, and to some extent the quality of the social environment, varying scenarios can occur. One scenario is inherent in Level II: without enough developmental potential, individuals return to primary integration. Other scenarios relate to individuals with sufficient developmental potential, progressing to Levels of the multilevel disintegration. It is possible that some individuals achieve Level III, remaining at that Level throughout life. Similarly, having reached Level IV the rare individual may achieve the apex of development, Level V. The theory also allows for elements of Level IV to occur in Level III, referred to as partial integrations. The important point is that we need to divest ourselves of any vestiges of stage theories when considering the levels of development.

Levels of development must by necessity be described separately, possibly creating an unintended consequence. When descriptions of each level are presented sequentially, it may give the impression that progression through the levels follows a linear, progressive sequence. Table 5 may reinforce the impression. Such representation suggests that a person with enough developmental potential progresses from primary integration to unilevel disintegration and so on, analogous to other stage theories of development such as those proposed by Piaget or Erikson, depicted in Table 6. But Dąbrowski took great pains to differentiate level from stage. He emphasized that a level is an identifiable developmental structure, not a structure that is a part of a universal, rigid hierarchical sequence which is associated with stage.

Table 6. Dąbrowski's Levels, Piaget's Stages and Erikson's Stages

Dabrowski	Piaget	Erikson
Secondary Integration	Formal operational	Ego Integrity vs. Despair
Organized Multilevel Disintegration	Concrete operational	Generativity vs. Stagnation
Spontaneous multilevel Disintegration	Preoperational	Intimacy vs. Isolation
Unilevel disintegration		Identity vs. Role Confusion
Primary integration	Sensorimotor	Industry vs. Inferiority
		Initiative vs. Guilt
		Autonomous vs. Shame
		Trust vs. Mistrust

A further difference between level and stage is that attainment of a level refers to a higher level replacing a lower one, not building upon it. However, even with this explanation, there remains the notion of linear progression: instead of stage, we have higher levels that replace lower ones in an invariant sequence. Dąbrowski does address this concern by indicating that two or more levels may coexist, though, as expected, they would exist in conflict. In my attempt to make sense of an individual's experience during Dąbrowskian development,

I propose that we say 'two or more levels DO coexist, rather than may coexist. Until Level IV (organized multilevel disintegration) is achieved completely, elements of primary integration remain in Levels II and III. During unilevel disintegration (Level II) the control of biology and environment continues unabated. Primary integration thinking and behavior persist in spontaneous multilevel disintegration (Level III) (see Figure 10).

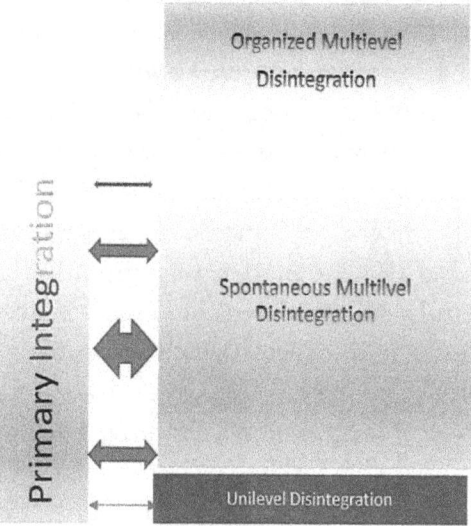

Figure 10. Level II and Level III Interactions with Primary Integration

In Figure 10, the four levels of development are presented, with primary integration as a separate element that exists alongside of Levels II and III. The interactions between the two Levels and primary integration increases until it disappears, indicated by its fading color. At that point, so does Level III begin to disappear, and we have the beginnings of Level IV (Level V is omitted because development continues with the attainment of Level IV). Neither primary integration nor Level III exist once Level IV is attained. The size and directionality of the arrows indicate the strength of the disintegrating processes. Level II has the bi-directional, narrow arrow to illustrate the weakness of the disintegrating process. All arrows in Level III illustrate intensification of disintegration, for which the level is known. As the disintegrating dynamisms emerge, their interaction with primary integration steadily increases until they reach their peak and then lessen in intensity as they destroy the primitive functioning, setting the stage for the fading of Level III.

Figure 10 illustrates my interpretation of Dąbrowski's statement that more than one level may exist simultaneously, but it does not explain my view of the interaction between Levels II and III and primary integration. What differentiates the two Levels from primary integration is the appearance of dynamisms. We cannot have disintegrating dynamisms operating without the coexistence of the characteristics of primary integration. *Individuals cannot progress from primary integration to unilevel and then to spontaneous multilevel disintegration by leaving primary integration behind.* Primitive functioning of primary integration is present until it is destroyed by the dynamisms of Level III. Put another way, primitive functioning is present until the fulsome attainment of Level IV. Take for example feelings of shame or guilt. These dynamisms cannot be activated unless individuals engage in evaluation of a behavior or thought that is felt to be unacceptable or immoral. Primitive function of primary integration is essential grist for the dynamism mill.

The coexistence of primary integration until Level IV is also consistent with Dąbrowski's proposition that the levels of development are not stages. Level III is not built on Level II; Level III is the prolongation of the disintegration that begins in Level II. Level III is not built on primary integration; Level III destroys it. However, it is not destroyed by a single action of dynamisms. As Dąbrowski states, there are no ages or time spans associated with the Levels. Dynamisms of disintegration erode the rigid mental organization of primary integration over time (as chemical and physical erosion gradually erode mountains). Individuals may remain at Level III for a very long time, implying that elements of primary integration coexist with Level III. It is the existence of aspects of primary integration that requires the activity of disintegrating dynamisms of Level III. Furthermore, elements of Level III and Level IV may coexist, illustrating what Dąbrowski terms partial disintegration, that is, reintegration at a higher level of only some mental structures, rather than the entire mental organization. While this is true, the primary interest here is interactions between primary integration and level III. Figure 10 addresses only the point that primary integration functioning coexists with the first two Levels of disintegration. The above discussion addresses the matter by explaining the important differences between level and stage.

Level IV: Resolution Not Disintegration. Another consideration regarding levels relates to the multilevel disintegration descriptor for Level IV. Recall that Level IV is bereft of the inner conflict of Level III. The creation of and adherence to a set of values serve to resolve the various manifestations of inner conflict. I contend that there is no disintegration in Level IV; as I noted earlier, resolution is the hallmark of this Level with the experience of tranquility, not inner conflict. I see some support for renaming Level IV in some of Dąbrowski's own words:

> *As the structure of level III is one of opposing and conflicting vertical forces, the structure of level IV is one of synthesis and increasing order of the organization of the inner psychic milieu and its activities. Inner conflicts abate while the unifying power of personality ideal increases in intensity.*
> (Dąbrowski, 1996, p.38)

The main mental activity at Level IV is not disintegration but rather personal transformation representing transcendence of biology and environment—the emergence of an autonomous, authentic self. I think that *self-directed resolution* or an equivalent term would be more consistent with such positive development than the current name of Level IV (*organized multilevel disintegration*).

CHAPTER 6
Emergence of Disintegrating Dynamisms: A Social-Cognitive Perspective

Dąbrowski identifies three groups of dynamisms, corresponding to the levels of development, namely, unilevel dynamisms (Level II), multilevel dynamisms (Level III & IV), and dynamisms of secondary integration (Level V) (Dąbrowski, 1970). Multilevel dynamisms include those defining both spontaneous and organized multilevel disintegration. Unilevel and spontaneous multilevel dynamisms are similar in that they function to destroy (disintegrate) primitive ways of thinking and behaving. Organized multilevel dynamisms and secondary integration dynamisms are expressions of advanced development. *Disintegrating* describes the unilevel and spontaneous multilevel dynamisms; *developmental* describes those that manifest advanced development.

How do disintegrating dynamisms emerge in daily living? While unilevel dynamisms—ambivalence and ambitendency—initiate the disintegration process, it is the "self" dynamisms of spontaneous multilevel disintegration that are responsible for the destruction of the mental organization of primary integration. The *self-dynamisms* of Level III include feelings of shame, astonishment with oneself, feelings of guilt, inferiority toward oneself, disquietude with oneself, and dissatisfaction with oneself. Dąbrowski uses various descriptors for these: *pathological, psychoneurotic dynamisms,* and *psychoneurotic symptoms* (Dąbrowski, 1970; 1972). I prefer *disintegrating* because it describes the essential role they play in the destruction of primitive ways of thinking and behaving.

It should be made clear that the descriptors "pathological" or "disintegrating" do not apply to all of the dynamisms in Level III. I exclude *inner conflict* because the self-dynamisms themselves involve such conflict. *Hierarchization* and *positive maladjustment* are not included because, by definition, they are positive cognitive and behavioral processes. Hierarchization, is defined in Dąbrowski's own words as:

> …*a recognition of higher and lower levels of experiences and phenomena. It is the beginning of sorting things out prior to the emergence of an autonomous hierarchy of values…. As a developmental factor, hierarchization is probably the least specific and the least differentiated of multilevel dynamisms.* (Dąbrowski, 1996, p. 35)

Hierarchization, then, is a cognitive process of classification of phenomena used in the creation of a hierarchy of values. The sorting process begins in Level III and extends into the subsequent levels. As such, it seems more appropriate to view it as a developmental rather than disintegrating dynamism.

Positive maladjustment is defined by Dąbrowski as:

> …*a conflict with and rejection of those standards and attitudes of one's social environment which are incompatible with one's growing awareness of higher values. The higher values as an autonomous and authentic hierarchy become an internal imperative. In its incipient form positive maladjustment may appear as a critical reaction and opposition to one's environment but without being accompanied by a clearly developed hierarchy of values.* (Dąbrowski, 1996, p. 36).

Inner conflict (noted earlier in Chapter 5) is a cognitive process characterized by awareness of discrepancies, which is not emotional but produces emotions. Rejection of standards and attitudes, as a cognitive process, can be manifested behaviorally. Analysis and criticism of, and opposition to, values of the social environment are initial manifestations of positive maladjustment. As it takes hold, this dynamism straddles Level III and IV.

Hierarchization and positive maladjustment are neither psychoneurotic symptoms nor disintegrating dynamisms; rather they represent the beginnings of re-integration at a higher level. In fact, hierarchization operates fully in Level IV and V and positive maladjustment is fully activated at the beginning of Level IV, signaling the emergence of the developmental dynamisms (Dąbrowski, 1996).

Dąbrowski on Emergence of Disintegrating Dynamisms

Disintegrating dynamisms emerge from overexcitability, the social environment and their interaction. Dąbrowski is explicit about the role of overexcitability in the rise of disintegrating dynamisms:

> *Psychic hyperexcitability [overexcitability] is one of the major developmental potentials, but it also forms a symptom, or a group of general psychoneurotic symptoms… Among the general psychoneurotic symptoms, we will discuss broadly the tendency to disquietude [a disintegrating dynamism]. Disquietude can arise with low, medium, or high psychological tension. What is the source of disquietude? It appears to be based, to a great extent, on psychic hyperexcitability, particularly of the emotional and the imaginational type.* (Dąbrowski, 1970, p. 40; italics and bracketed remarks added)

Disquietude with oneself is used as an example to explain that psychoneurotic symptoms—disintegrating dynamisms—arise from overexcitability. Dąbrowski's emphasis on two forms of overexcitability—emotional and imaginational—as sources for dynamisms, suggests that all five forms of overexcitability are present to generate dynamisms. Interaction among the higher (intellectual, imaginational, and emotional) and lower (sensual and psychomotor) forms, according to Dąbrowski, creates inner conflict. The conflict created by the presence of the five forms "precipitates psychoneurotic processes" (1970, p. 38), or in my terms, disintegrating dynamisms.

The theory also proposes that the social environment plays an important role in development. Developmental potential, in particular its component of overexcitability, combined with a favorable environment, leads to advanced development. The social environment contributes to development, and therefore to the rise of dynamisms. Dąbrowski (1970) provides an unexpected explanation regarding how this occurs. To paraphrase: *Contrary to common perception of the developmental process, Dąbrowskian development cannot occur when the social environment is such that youth have complete fulfillment of their basic needs in an environment providing feelings of complete security*. Partial satisfaction of children's needs—frustration—is said to contribute to the emergence of higher needs and emotions, that is, of dynamisms. Dąbrowski believes strongly in this assertion. Since this view of the social environment is likely to be controversial, I add Dąbrowski's own words:

> *Positive inner psychic transformation occurs where children and youth do not have all the things necessary to fulfill all their basic needs and where conditions do not lead to the feeling of complete security. This transformation is more likely to occur where the individuals have only partial satisfaction of their basic needs and where stimuli exist which provoke at least partial dissatisfaction, hierarchization and postulation of an ideal.*
>
> *[Dąbrowski] wishes to emphasize that, in his opinion, such transformations cannot take place when there is complete security, and when all basic needs have been satisfied. For the development of higher needs and higher emotions, it is necessary to have partial frustrations, some inner conflicts, some deficits in basic needs, some difficulties in the realization of the needs arising from the biological life cycle. Higher needs must be stimulated and cultivated simultaneously with the care given to the so-called basic needs.* (Dąbrowski, 1970, p. 35)

The point Dąbrowski is making, in my view, is that a social environment (e.g., a family environment) that provides all the needs and wants of youth is not facilitative of development. To be frank, parents who spoil their children by granting them all they desire are not facilitators of development; in fact, such parenting reinforces impulsivity rather than growth. Thus, parents should provide experiences of "partial frustration", which means not acquiescing to every childish desire but rather providing just for children's *basic* needs. Experience of partial frustration is an important contributor to development, and therefore, to the emergence of dynamisms. Here we have another of Dąbrowski's counter-intuitive proposition contrary to popular belief, frustration, even continually experienced, can be *positive*. However, this is premised on an individual's having sufficient endowment of developmental potential manifested by dynamisms: "It is clear to us that continuous frustration without the corresponding development of inner psychic transformation, self-awareness and self-control, will have a negative outcome" (Dąbrowski, 1970, p. 38). In the same citation, Dąbrowski goes one step further regarding frustration. Again, contrary to the widely held view, low frustration tolerance, rather than high, is an indicator of developmental potential. Dąbrowski not only states that low frustration tolerance is associated with highly sensitive, creative people but also adds that high frustration tolerance is "characteristic of psychopaths" (Dąbrowski, 1970, p. 38). Individuals endowed with developmental potential, therefore, tend to have low frustration tolerance. Sufficient developmental potential, and a social environment that produces some frustration of other than basic needs contribute to the rise of disintegrating dynamisms. Overexcitability, in its five forms, combined with a particular type of social environment, is the source of disintegrating dynamisms.

Assuming the presence of overexcitability and an appropriate social environment, we seek to understand *specifically* how disintegrating dynamisms emerge. A potential answer requires reframing *disintegrating dynamisms of spontaneous multilevel disintegration* as *negative emotions*. It is not without a sense of irony that I use the word *reframing*, as I discuss an aspect of a theory famous for its reframing of constructs. Though feelings of shame, guilt and so on, are properly called dynamisms in the theory of positive disintegration, the label "dynamism" obscures an obvious fact: shame, guilt, and dissatisfaction are negative emotions. It likely seems pedantic, if not facetious, to readers that I feel it necessary to use "reframing disintegrating dynamism" as negative emotions instead of simply stating so. After all, they actually are negative emotions. However, the theory of positive disintegration has a powerful effect, at times unconscious, on its advocates. It is as if we impose an impenetrable aura surrounding the theory creating an impression that any departure from the official lexicon is seen as tampering with the theory. Of course, calling disintegrating dynamisms negative emotions has no bearing on the coherence of the theory. In a sense, shame, guilt and so on were reframed by Dąbrowski as dynamisms. Here, I reverse the reframing while retaining Dąbrowski's meaning.

Thinking of 'disintegrating dynamisms as 'negative emotions' revises the question of their emergence: How do *negative emotions* arise in daily life? An answer should apply to negative emotions in general, including those termed *disintegrating dynamisms*. The theory of positive disintegration has no explicit conceptualization of emotion, and therefore cannot be used to answer the question. There exists a plethora of conceptions of emotion, ranging from the James-Lang theory from the beginning of the last century to the more recent concept of *emotional intelligence* by Salovey and Mayer (1990). A promising answer to the question lies in the works of Theodore Kemper and Richard Lazarus, representing a sociological and a social psychological approach, respectively. Taken together, their theorizing forms a *social-cognitive theory of emotion*. Application of that socially oriented theory to disintegrating dynamisms suggests an explanation for their day-to-day emergence.

Kemper's Social Interactional Theory

Kemper (1978) observed that, while sociologists had not entirely neglected the construct of emotion, its systematic study was found primarily in the field of psychology. He lamented that of the many available theories of emotion, "none is specifically sociological" (p. 32). Kemper concluded that emphasis on social interaction and social relationships were requirements of a sociological theory of emotion, yielding his *social interactional theory* (SIT) (1978, 1991, 2006). SIT is premised on the assumption that emotions are better understood as outcomes or products of various types of social relationships:

> *The most important premise of any sociological theory of emotions must be that an extremely large class of human emotions results from real, anticipated, imagined, or recollected outcomes of social relationships: 'she says she does not love me'; 'he says I did a good job'; 'I claimed to be honest, but was caught in a lie'; 'he obligated himself to me, but then reneged'; and so forth. These are outcomes of social relationships that ought to stimulate emotion.* (Kemper, 1978, p. 32)

Kemper proposed that human emotions are, by and large, responses to environmental events, particularly social relations, because they "are the most important part of the environment" (Kemper, 1991, p. 330). In effect, social relations are the context in which emotions are produced. Four types of social relations may stimulate emotions: real, anticipated, imagined, or recollected. That emotions arise during *real* social interactions is a truism. It may not be as obvious that the other three types—anticipated, imagined, and recollected—also lead to emotions. According to Kemper, we can create emotions ourselves through conjuring up specific social events. We can experience emotions by anticipating and imagining future events, an experience of anxiety as students anticipate a failing grade on a future test. Psychologically, this is a familiar scenario, commonly termed *test anxiety* or *anticipatory anxiety*. Seen through a Kemperian lens, though, a student's experience of anxiety is a response to an *imagined* negative social outcome in one or more social relationships, for example, the parent-child relationship. Anxiety is the result of an *anticipated OR imaginary* social outcome: "If I fail, my parents will be very disappointed with me." In addition to *real, anticipated* and *imagined* social situations that produce emotions, Kemper draws attention to a fourth type: *recollected* or *recalled*. As we have all experienced, the mental review of interactions with others after the fact has the potential to spark emotions, especially when the outcome of those interactions was negative. Kemper, in adding *recollected* to his outcomes of social relations, identifies a common human process which often occurs late in the evening—that of reviewing of social interactions of the day, at times resulting in negative emotions that may interferes with sleep.

Kemper's SIT (social interactional theory) is a *sociological* theory of emotions, explaining how the outcomes of social relationships of various kinds result in human emotions. However, it seems that the theory is not only *sociological*, but also implicitly *psychological*. As a psychologist I cannot conceive of how outcomes of social relationships can result in emotions without cognitive processing of the outcome. Outcomes need to be interpreted in a particular way for emotions to result. Without interpretation, "She says she does not love me" is merely a factual, neutral statement. Kemper's theory draws attention to the importance of social relationships for understanding emotions, complementing the predominance of psychological theories which emphasize cognitive processing in the experience of emotions.

Lazarus's Social Psychological Theory

Richard Lazarus is likely best known for his pioneering contribution to our understanding of stress and coping (e.g., Lazarus, 1966). Perhaps less well known is Lazarus's cognitive-motivational-relational theory of emotion (Lazarus, 1993, 2006), which I call *social psychological*. Of the three constructs in his theory, cognition predominates, given his proposition that it causes emotion. Lazarus (1991) was emphatic that cognition is both a sufficient and necessary condition for emotions to occur. He explained that sufficient means that "thoughts can produce emotions; *necessary* means that emotions cannot occur without thought" (italics in original, p. 353). Specifically, it is the cognitive process of appraisal that causes emotion.

> *Appraisal is an evaluation of the significance of knowledge about what is happening for our personal well-being. Only the recognition that we have something to gain or lose, that is, that the outcome of a transaction is relevant to goals and well-being, generates an emotion* (italics in original, 1991, p. 352).

Emotion, negative or positive, is produced when we evaluate an event as threatening to or enhancing our personal well-being, respectively. If an event is appraised as irrelevant to our well-being, the result is no emotion. Personality factors contribute to the appraisal process. Lazarus (2006) identified several personality factors including personal goals, beliefs about self, physical and social attractiveness, intelligence, social skills, health, energy level, education, and wealth. Personality factors affect the quality of appraisal, and therefore, contribute to the experience of emotion or lack thereof.

Lazarus's theory assumes a bidirectional relationship between cognition and emotion: emotion also influences cognition. Emotion not only has the potential to impair logical thought, but also has the power to stimulate additional appraisal and, therefore, emotion:

> *The moment an emotion occurs it becomes food, so to speak, for the next appraisal and emotion. Thus, if we feel ashamed by having been made angry because we regard anger as an unwarranted personal lapse, the anger could be said to have generated the shame.* (p. 353).

In Lazarus's example, anger is the product of appraisal of an event; shame is the product of a second appraisal of the emotion of anger. Implied in the second appraisal is a set of personal standards used to appraise one's experience of anger. Judgment of anger as a "lapse"—a violation of our standards—causes the experiencing of a second emotion, shame.

Lazarus's approach is not simply a cognitive mediation model of emotion. Like Kemper, Lazarus's conceptualization of emotion includes social interaction as a core element in the emotion creation process. His emphasis on social interaction is evident in his description of his theory and the influences on the process of appraisal.

> *I [Lazarus] refer to my approach to stress and the emotions as cognitive, motivational, and relational because, as I see it, these processes lie at the heart of all our lives. The term relational means that emotional ways depend on what transpires between a person and the environment, which most importantly consists of other persons. Another essential*

premise is that we are constantly appraising—that is, imputing relational meaning to our ongoing and changing relationships with others and the physical environment, and it is this meaning that shapes and defines our emotions. (Lazarus, 2006, p. 9-10)

Taken together, Kemper's and Lazarus's core propositions form the constituents of my social-cognitive theory of emotions. While Lazarus emphasizes the role of cognition, the theories converge in the view that social interactions and social relationships are the essential arenas in which emotions are produced.

Summary. A social-cognitive theory of emotions is grounded in Kemper's *sociological* and R.S. Lazarus's *social psychological* perspectives. In the *social interaction* theory of emotion, emotions are the outcome of social relationships marked by streams of interactions with others in individuals' environments. All outcomes of the four types of social relations—real, imaginary, anticipated or recollected— can produce emotions in individuals. In the *social psychological* theory of emotion, emotions are caused by cognition, specifically by appraisals of events in the environment, with particular emphasis on the social environment. Emotions are the result of appraisals or judgments of events in terms of their impact on personal well-being. Appraisals of threat to well-being produce negative emotions; appraisals of enhancement of well-being produce positive emotions. Like Kemper, Lazarus proposed that emotions occur in a social interactive context; that is, emotions have their origins in social interactions. Cognition in the form of appraisal causes emotion; emotion in turn affects cognition. In short, most of the emotions we experience relate to our appraisal of our involvement with other people: cognition and emotion are not separate but interrelated.

Social-Cognitive Theory of Emotion

From a social-cognitive perspective, emotions are caused by our appraisals of social environmental interactions. However, emotions are also experienced in interactions with the physical environment, such as the positive emotion of being awestruck when looking at the Milky Way or when witnessing a sunset on ocean waters. Similarly, we may experience negative emotions when we encounter a bear on a hike. Nonetheless, it is safe to say that most emotions experienced day to day are those that implicate other people, especially those with whom we have some degree of relationship. These are the emotions of primary concern in this chapter. In Kemper's SIT, emotions are the outcomes of social relations, which may be imaginary, anticipated, real, or recollected. This variety of contexts suggest that there are countless opportunities for experiencing emotions. The intensity of those emotions will vary but their sheer number is large. How many times a day do we imagine scenarios and anticipate events that include a veritable cast of characters in our lives? It is likely that we will conjure up various situations that may relate to work, other personal circumstances, and of course, relationships. Perhaps less frequently—though likely more important—we experience emotions during real social interactions. Furthermore, emotions occur because of recalling actual situations, particularly when they themselves were laden with emotion. The four types of social contexts have one thing in common: when emotions are experienced, they are the product of appraisals—our judgment of their impact on our personal well-being.

The social-cognitive view of emotions, with its emphasis on appraisal, is contrary to the commonly held view that events themselves cause emotion (See Table 7).

Table 7. Common and social cognitive views of emotion using anger as an example.

Common sense	Social-Cognitive
Event ⟶ Emotion	Event ⟵ Appraisal ⟶ Emotion

To illustrate the process of appraisal, I select a short-lived scenario involving the interaction of two participants in an intimate relationship. *Event* represents the behavior of Participant A, and Participant B experiences emotion; the selected emotion is *anger*, because we are concerned with negative emotions in this chapter. Let us consider the rise of B's anger as A and B interact regarding a First World task, loading the dishwasher (readers may select their own anger scenario, though my chosen task is a surprisingly common source of conflict for partners in a relationship). B had previously loaded the dishwasher and sees A rearranging the items, an often-occurring event in their relationship. B is more than irritated and says: "You make me so angry!" B's statement illustrates the common-sense view of how emotions arise: if it were not for A's behavior, B would not feel anger. From a social-cognitive point of view, B's exclamation is incorrect. (A, possibly a psychologist, may know this but it is not the time to explain it to B!). B has appraised A's behavior as a threat to psychological well-being, thereby creating the anger. How can rearranging items in a dishwasher be judged a threat to one's well-being? Of course, the answer lies in the appraisal of the behavior, not the behavior itself. As Lazarus noted many factors affect the appraisal process. In the dishwasher scenario, B may feel insecure in the relationship and has interpreted A's behavior as intentional provocation, as criticism, or that B is unimportant to A, and so on, all of which pose threats to the quality of relationship, and therefore to personal well-being. If B changes the appraisal of the event, then anger is no longer created, for example, "Isn't it funny that A needs to do that!", "There A goes again; you'd think A is OCD!", or "I guess it's okay to have different perspectives on the best way to do this". Changing appraisals is not an easy task because in this case, B would have to become more secure in the relationship. Ultimately, B would have to understand and accept that it is the appraisal that is causing the anger.

The common-sense view of emotion experiencing is quite entrenched. The reason may be that the cognitive processing of events is so fast that we are not readily aware that we are appraising others' behaviors. Ironically, the smarter the people (and therefore, more prone to rapid processing of information), the more difficult it is to convince them that they are creating their emotions due to the way they appraise social interactive events.

Appraisal. For Lazarus, appraisal is a multidimensional factor composed of the personality attributes of participants in social interactions and the history of their relationships. In my approach to appraisal, I have found three aspects to be particularly influential of the process: intelligence, history, and self-efficacy related to events, represented in Figure 11.

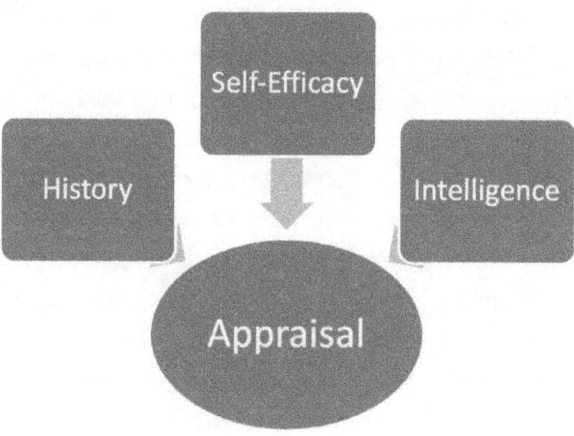

Figure 11. Factors affecting the appraisal process

Individual differences in these variables affect the emotion-generating process. Level of general intelligence influences the mental ability of awareness. Heightened awareness results in a greater perception of aspects of a situation—increased consciousness of the nuances and subtleties of an event—and so affects the creation of and intensity of emotion experience. Level of intelligence also affects the speed with which appraisal occurs. Rapid processing of data is generally an asset for individuals with high intelligence. Rapid processing of social interactive events, however, has its potential psychological hazards. Fast processing may result in overlooked cues and may lead to distortion of events producing spurious negative emotions. History with the social situation also affects intensity.

History includes both the history that participants share and the novelty of social situations. In the dishwasher example, B's irritation was transformed into anger because of the history of the situation. Newly encountered situations may be perceived as more threatening, or alternatively be more self-aggrandizing than habitual ones. Consider a first job interview. As one anticipates the upcoming interview, its novelty will likely lead the job seeker to postulate a series of potential events (e.g., failing to answer questions appropriately; disapproval from the interviewer), and appraise these as threatening to acquiring the job, resulting in anxiety. As the number of job interviews increases—as novelty decreases—intensity of anxiety is lowered. On the other hand, an employee receiving unexpected praise for job performance will probably interpret it as enhancing well-being, producing a happy emotion: intensity of positive emotion lessens when praise is continuous.

Lastly, self-efficacy is a moderating variable determining not only intensity but also whether an emotion is created. Self-efficacy, rather than self-esteem, affects appraisal because it refers to one's level of esteem or confidence with respect to performing in a specific role or task. Returning to the dishwasher scenario, a contributing factor to the creation of anger was B's feelings of insecurity in the relationship. B's low self-efficacy with respect to relationship with A influenced B's self-appraisal which found a threat to well-being. In contrast, if B possessed high self-efficacy regarding the relationship, it is unlikely that emotion would have been created. At the very least, high self-efficacy would have created irritation, rather than anger. Feelings of self-efficacy during stimulus events contributes to the production of positive emotion or virtually no emotion. On the other hand, lack of self-efficacy may lead to appraisal of events as psychologically threatening, thereby creating negative emotions. In line with Lazarus's view, personality factors of intelligence and self-efficacy, combined with history, determine the valence of appraisal in various social milieus.

Social situations. As a reminder, Kemper stated that emotions result from real, anticipated, imagined, or recollected *outcomes* of social relationships. In my social cognitive theory, I have replaced *outcomes* with *social milieux* or *situations*. Outcomes, as I noted earlier, suggest interpretation of events in a social relation: outcomes are the product of cognitive processing, distinct from the situations themselves. The four types of social situations include events that may be used to create emotions. Events are typically the behaviors of participants involved in an interaction. The dishwasher scenario is an example of a *real* social situation in which observed behavior is appraised as a threat to personal well-being. *Imaginary* and *anticipated* social situations are, by definition, strictly mental constructions, although the emotions they can produce are real. *Recollected* social situations refers to the recall of real social situations in which emotions were experienced. We are likely to recall situations that are marked by negative emotions; revisiting these situations tends to provoke thinking and analysis, which may interfere with sleep. When compared with the other types of situations, recollected ones are unique because they have the power to add emotions to those originally experienced. Figure 12 is a schematic illustration of how additional emotions are created.

Figure 13 Emotion Outcome of Recall of Anger Scenario

A's Rearrangement of dishes← B's Appraisal→Threat→ Anger← B's Appraisal 2 →Threat→Shame

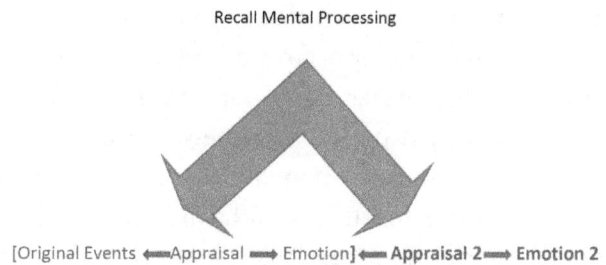

Figure 12. Emotion Outcome of Recalling Real Social Situation

Recall of a social situation includes reviewing the behavior of the participants and the emotion experienced in the situation. Specifically, the other participant's behavior was appraised in the past situation, and an emotion—positive or negative—was the outcome. A second appraisal occurs, and a second emotion is generated. If the emotion in the real scenario was positive, the second appraisal will likely be positive. Since we are concerned with negative emotions in this chapter, I will use the dishwasher example to elaborate on the recall process, illustrated in Figure 13.

A's Rearrangement of dishes← B's Appraisal→Threat→ Anger← B's Appraisal 2 →Threat→Shame

Figure 13. Emotion Outcome of Recall of Anger Scenario

While B recalls the entire situation, I propose that the second appraisal focuses on the emotion of anger. B experiences shame because she believes that one should not get so angry in the face of a trivial matter. In the actual situation, A's behavior was the focus of B's appraisal; in recall, it is anger experienced in the initial situation that is the focus of B's appraisal. One or more of the factors influencing appraisal (e.g., intelligence, self-efficacy, and history) can explain appraisal in the actual situation. To understand the experience of shame, we need to add another dimension: *standards of behavior*. B's feeling ashamed is created by the awareness that experiencing and expressing such anger violates a standard that is part of B's self-perception. B will have thoughts such as "Why did I get so angry? What's wrong with me? Getting so upset about nothing!!"

There is an important distinction to be made between the kinds of emotion that the above description illustrates. Emotion in the real situation is directed externally; in the recall situation, it is directed internally. Shame, then, is an example of internally directed emotion.

Motivations for Recalling Social Situations

We began this chapter by asking how disintegrating dynamisms emerge in daily life.

My proposed answer lies in an elaboration of the recollected social situations as described above. To make the answer explicit, we need to address another dimension of recollection: motivation. When individuals engage in recall, what motivates them to do so?

It is safe to say that some, if not many, individuals reflect on social interactions after they occur, particularly when interactions are fraught with emotion. As with other psychological characteristics and processes, there are individual differences in motivation for engaging in recall of events. My understanding of the differences in motivation indicates that there are at least four motives: defensiveness, social anxiety, conformity, and self-understanding. We may experience all four forms from time to time as we engage in the recall of social situations.

Motivated by *defensiveness*, our aim is to find re-assurance that our negative emotion, in our example, anger, is justified. When we are motivated by defensiveness, we recall the details of the interaction that led up to our reaction of anger, with particular attention to the other person's behavior. Conceiving of the other person's antecedent behaviors as causes of our emotions, we blame the other person for our anger. We may conclude that "anybody would get angry in response to that behavior!" With little or no attention to ourselves, appraisal of our anger likely rekindles it. Standards of behavior are not part of the mental processing of the original situation. In effect, defensive recall simply adds justification to the commonsense view of emotion—"The other person made me angry" and "I was right to be angry."

When the motivation is *social anxiety*, additional emotion is expected during recall. While socialization tends to condition us to seek approval and avoid disapproval, there are individuals in whom this condition is highly magnified. Social anxiety motivates individuals to spend a great deal of time and energy thinking about social events. Thinking of future social interactions creates anticipatory anxiety of such proportion that it results in avoidance of future situations. Such analysis is predictably more intricate and intense when the social interaction is emotionally laden. In recall of social situations motivated by social anxiety, behavior of self and others is viewed through a dark lens, a highly self-critical, self-fulfilling-prophecy point of view. When motivated by anxiety, recalling a social situation in which anger is expressed would likely be a devastating experience. The recall may focus largely on the other party, listing their verbal and nonverbal cues, and, as in the actual situation, erroneously interpreting the components of the interaction as criticism and disapproval. When the focus is on oneself, it is highly self-critical, ending in a resolve to avoid future social events. Recall of social interactions tends to be used to confirm one's negative self-efficacy in social situations and to reinforce one's use of avoidance to cope with intense social anxiety.

When motivation is *conformity*, there will likely be self-directed emotions generated by the recall. As a result of socialization, we are expected to conform to societal standards, which are learned largely through child rearing practices and other societal institutions. Any breach of standards will lead to a fear of punishment—not necessarily physical, but rather in the form of disapproval, real or anticipated. There are norms regarding the emotion of anger and its socially appropriate forms of expression. For the anger scenario, a socially appropriate response would be something like: "It is irritating when you rearrange the dishes. I wish that you would stop doing it," said in a mildly irritated tone. Subsequently, individuals may automatically feel guilty once their own emotions calm, enabling them to realize that though their response was socially appropriate, their tone conveyed their anger. If feelings, such as guilt and embarrassment, are experienced, it is because of fear of punishment, in the form of disapproval, for contravening an internalized social norm. Concerns raised by reflection relate to self, not the other party in the interaction. In short, during recall we appraise the emotion of anger, viewing it as contravening a standard of behavior (a conformity), creating an internally directed emotion such as guilt, and perhaps even anxiety if we anticipate disapproval.

Self-understanding is similar to conformity, with important differences. Both of these forms of recall focus primarily on *self* rather than the other participant in the interaction, appraising the emotion in the original situation using standards of behavior. In fact, the resulting emotion may be identical, such as feeling guilt or shame caused by a realization that standards of behavior have been broken. The significant difference between self-*understanding* and *conformity* is the reason for experiencing the ensuing emotions. In conformity motivation recall, the emotion of guilt or shame is created by the fear of punishment in the form of disapproval. In self-understanding, the same emotions are created by other considerations. The aim of self-understanding motivation, as the name implies, seeks to answer questions such as "I know the behavior was irritating but it was about something so trivial; why did I overreact?" "I feel terrible about this whole thing. I know that I shouldn't react so intensely. What was going on in me at the time?" "This must have hurt the person, what can I do next time?"

In short, the aim of self-understanding is self-improvement. Social anxiety, conformity, and self-understanding, as differing motivations to recollect social situations, may produce the same emotions, such as guilt, shame, or anxiety. However, *in Dąbrowski's theory, it is not the emotions themselves that matter, it is the rationale involved in their construction.*

Application to Disintegrating Dynamisms

From the social-cognitive perspective on emotions, disintegrating dynamisms are a special case of negative emotions produced by multiple appraisals of actual and recalled social interactions. Both types of interactions are required because actual events are fodder for additional appraisal. There is an important difference between the emotions produced in actual events and those produced in recalled events. Appraisals occurring *in vivo* (actual events) produce emotions that are aimed externally. In the dishwasher anger scenario, the negative emotion produced is directed externally, whereas appraisal during the *recall* of the event produces emotions that are *directed at self*. Negative emotions produced by guilt, shame, and anxiety (three of four motivation types) are not directed externally. Guilt, shame, and anxiety are self-referent negative emotions, created by reflecting and interpreting behavior observed in oneself and in others in *recalled* interactions. Apart from the emotions produced by defensive motivation (the fourth type), emotions produced by guilt, shame, and anxiety are self-referent negative emotions. What makes disintegrating dynamism special is not that they are self-referent negative emotions: rather, it is the *type* of motivation which guides appraisal of events. Self-understanding is qualitatively different, and arguably of greater value to personal development than, say, defensiveness. In the theory of positive disintegration, the mental processing of events using the social cognitive framework of emotion is associated with developmental potential.

I can now propose an answer to the question: How do disintegrating dynamisms arise in daily life? Disintegrating dynamisms, as negative emotions, do not just arise, they are created by appraisal performed by individuals motivated by self-understanding, an outcome of sufficient developmental potential. The analysis of recalled social interactions is the *beginning* of the emergence of dynamisms in daily life, associated with the beginning of Level III. As spontaneous disintegration progresses, self-analysis proceeds from *requiring* external stimuli, to spontaneous reflection *independent* of external stimuli. In other words, individuals' own thoughts, in addition to recalled social interactions, become events that are appraised.

This is consistent with Dąbrowskian perspective in general and with Level III dynamisms. In the theory of positive disintegration, when development occurs it typically begins with a maturational milestone or an environmental event—that is, events that are beyond an individuals' control. For example, puberty or death of a loved one serve to launch developmental processes. More to the point, Level III, in which disintegrating dynamisms reside, is termed spontaneous multilevel disintegration. In common usage *spontaneous* is synonymous with terms such as unplanned or impulsive; Dąbrowski used it to indicate that the impetus for change comes from responding to experiences, rather than from within. Individuals at this level of development are, in effect, in a reactive mode, beginning with their reacting to social environmental events. However, from a social-cognitive point of view, the events in and of themselves are not enough to explain the emergence of dynamisms; the critical component implicit in the theory of positive disintegration is the cognitive processing of events: disintegrating dynamisms are negative emotions, created initially by appraisal of recalled social interactions.

It is the experience of social interactions characterized by negative emotions that is the common motivator for individuals to recall and interpret those events. I proposed four types of motivation to conduct the mental processing of such events. The highest motivation, persistent self-understanding, is associated with individuals that have developmental potential. However, it is unlikely that individuals so endowed begin their processing of social events with persistent self-understanding; it is likely that a lower form appears first. This is consistent with the general idea of the theory that lower forms are replaced by higher ones.

Disintegrating Dynamisms: Self Referent Negative Emotions

I have used social interactions that involve the negative emotion of anger, though they could also involve recall of any social interaction that include emotions such as sadness or disappointment. From a Dąbrowskian point of view, the motivation to recall social interactions, whether they are laden with negative emotions or not, can be categorized into lower and higher forms: defensiveness, conformity, social anxiety, and self-understanding. I theorize that individuals who routinely recall social interactions motivated by self-understanding are most likely to be endowed with developmental potential. At first, individuals may variously experience all four motivations. When recall of social events for the purpose of self-understanding becomes dominant, the negative emotions produced are the disintegrating dynamisms of Level III: spontaneous multilevel disintegration.

In conclusion, disintegrating dynamisms as negative emotions do not simply arise—they are generated by persons who possess enough developmental potential to be prone to reflecting on their behaviors in social interactions. Cognitive processing of recalled events is motivated by self-understanding. Appraisal of recalled events focuses on an individual's own behaviors rather than those of other participants. *Disintegrating dynamisms are a special case of self-directed negative emotions, produced by awareness of a discrepancy between one's behavior and one's values.*

Chapter 7
Emergence of Developmental Dynamisms

In contemplating the nature of developmental dynamisms, the question in the previous chapter regarding *disintegrating* dynamisms is equally applicable to *developmental* dynamisms. How do dynamisms, in general, arise in day-to-day life? To address the question regarding disintegrating dynamisms, it is necessary to apply a conceptual framework (a social-cognitive theory of emotion) external to the theory of positive disintegration. In contrast, an answer to the question concerning the rise of developmental dynamisms is found in the theory of positive disintegration itself. Before providing clarification of their emergence, it is important to note which dynamisms I include under the rubric "developmental" because I propose a few additions.

In Chapter 6, I proposed re-assigning two Level III dynamisms, positive maladjustment and hierarchization, from the disintegrating category to the developmental category. My rationale was based on the fact that the hallmark of Level III is inner conflict, and that these two dynamisms represent advances in development rather than destruction of lower forms of being. In addition to positive maladjustment and hierarchization, I add creative instinct, which is said to occupy more than one level. *Creative instinct* is a dynamism "which discovers and molds new forms of reality." (Dąbrowski, 1973, p. 27). This instinct is associated with motivation for artistic expression and may lead to productivity in literary, visual, and performing arts. In my view, none of the three dynamisms noted above (positive maladjustment, hierarchization, and creative instinct) would be aptly described as "disintegrating" or "pathological" (see Chapter 6).

In the theory of positive disintegration, developmental dynamisms occur across Levels IV and V. Level IV dynamisms include *subject object in oneself, empathy, third factor, inner psychic transformation, self-awareness, self-control, education-of-oneself, and autopsychotherapy.* Level IV/V dynamisms are those dynamisms that are active at the borderline of organized multilevel disintegration (IV) and secondary integration (V), namely, *responsibility for self and others, authentism, autonomy, and personality ideal.* While personality ideal is included above, it is the only dynamism defining Level V.

There are significant differences between disintegrating and developmental dynamisms (see Table 8). Distinctions between the two types of dynamism define their respective levels of development.

Table 8. Multilevel Dynamisms: Disintegrating and Developmental

Dynamism Type	Level of Development	Defining Characteristic	Operation	Multilevelness
Disintegrating	III	Self-oriented negative emotions	Response to stimuli; isolated	Growing Awareness of Lower and Higher Forms
Developmental	IV and V	Advanced mental growth	Inner directed; collaborative	Adherence to higher; rejection of lower

Disintegrating dynamisms occur in Level III (*spontaneous* multilevel disintegration). Level III is *multilevel* because there is a growing awareness of the difference between lower and higher thinking and behaving. As constituents of that level, disintegrating dynamisms are unplanned emotional responses to specific internal (e.g., maturational) and external (e.g., social interactional) environmental stimuli. As such, the dynamisms tend to operate in an isolated manner, creating experiences of inner conflict. In Level III, development occurs in response to environmental stimuli. In contrast, developmental dynamisms occur in Level IV (*organized* multilevel disintegration). Dąbrowski used *organized*, meaning directed, to denote that development in Level IV is directed by—under the control of—individuals.

While disintegrating dynamisms are in effect negative emotions, developmental dynamisms are positive, value-laden, advanced cognitive processes. Furthermore, level of organization is a criterion that distinguishes the two categories. Developmental dynamisms work in a coordinated fashion. In fact, there are specific dynamisms, such as the third factor (autonomy), that are designated to oversee the collaboration among them. Developmental dynamisms define Level IV as a phase of *advanced* development. The multilevel descriptor of that level indicates a commitment to adhere to the higher ways of thinking and behaving, while rejecting the lower forms. In my use of the term developmental dynamisms, I include what Dąbrowski refers to as the dynamisms of Level IV/V and Level V. Level V dynamisms define the full achievement of the highest level of human development.

Emergence of Developmental Dynamisms

The explanation of the emergence of developmental dynamisms lies in developmental potential. Recall that, in his description of developmental potential, Dąbrowski noted that it is manifested in overexcitability, special abilities and talents, and the third factor, autonomy (Dąbrowski, 1970). Clearly, the word *factors* means dynamisms; a synonym for autonomous is *self-directed*, which defines the concept of *organized* in Level IV organized multilevel disintegration. Developmental dynamisms, not the disintegrating dynamisms, are the "autonomous inner forces" that are part of developmental potential. In addition to a simple semantic argument, the theory supports my conclusion. Disintegrating dynamisms in Level III are the product of an individual's responses, largely to events of the maturation process and/or in the social environment. Puberty, academic failure, or loss of employment can trigger the process of disintegration. Assuming enough developmental potential, the awakening that occurs can activate disintegrating dynamisms. These are not, strictly speaking, autonomous and can be accounted for by the five forms of overexcitability. Possession of the five forms produces conflict, as, for example, sensual pulls in a selfish direction and emotional pulls in an altruist direction. A closer examination of the two types of dynamisms adds support for my proposal that only the developmental type represent autonomous inner forces.

From Developmental Potential to Developmental Dynamisms

If the theory of positive disintegration were merely another stage theory, the answer to the question of how developmental dynamisms emerge would be simple: higher order developmental dynamisms simply build on the lower disintegrating dynamisms. However, the theory of positive disintegration is not a typical stage theory of development in which advanced forms emerge from more primitive ones in a linear, sequential fashion. According to Dąbrowski, when developmental dynamisms appear and take hold, disintegrating dynamisms themselves are eradicated. The negative self-dynamisms, such as inferiority toward oneself or dissatisfaction with oneself, are themselves destroyed and replaced by, for example, subject-object in oneself, self-awareness, self-control and authentism. By destroying lower thinking and behavior patterns, disintegrating dynamisms are essential for the emergence of developmental dynamisms; *but disintegrating dynamisms do not create them*. Developmental dynamisms do not build on the former ones, they arise as distinct processes.

In providing an explanation for the rise of developmental dynamisms, we need to recall that the two groups of dynamisms discussed in Chapter 6 and the current chapter are inextricably bound to levels of development. Disintegrating dynamisms are indistinguishable from Level III; similarly, developmental dynamisms cannot be distinguished from Level IV. The two multilevel disintegration parts of development are defined by their respective dynamisms. Dąbrowski noted that movement from one level to another cannot be termed *transition* because the higher level does not evolve from the lower one. To explain movement from lower to higher, Dąbrowski used his concept of developmental potential. Developmental potential is essential for advanced development. the level of one's endowment of developmental potential sets a ceiling on Dąbrowski's definition of development. Movement from Level III—disintegrating dynamisms—to Level IV—developmental dynamisms—then, is explained by a generous endowment of developmental potential. Dąbrowski argues that Level IV dynamisms, made possible by developmental potential, were present in embryonic form within individuals. This explanation is consistent with his definition of developmental potential, which includes the nuclei of autonomous inner forces, most notably the third factor. Before these inherent dynamisms can be unleashed, lower forms of thinking and behaving—products of biology and socialization—need to be destroyed, hence the need for the disintegrating dynamisms. The seeds of emergent developmental dynamisms are innate from birth, and the forces of biology and socialization act as barriers, interfering with their expression.

Developmental potential, with its nuclei of developmental dynamisms, explains that these dynamisms do not build upon, evolve, or otherwise arise from the lower disintegrating dynamisms. However, the question remains: how do dynamisms, such as self-control, identification, and empathy, among others, arise in daily experience? An answer to the question is provided by Dąbrowski's description of two examples of *partial disintegration* and *partial secondary integration* (Dąbrowski, 1970). Partial disintegration refers to the destruction of discrete occurrences of primary integrated mental structure, thereby influencing thought and behavior. Partial secondary integration refers to replacing the primitive structure with one that is higher in terms of complexity and morality. Both processes describe the actions of the two different types of dynamisms.

> *What is partial disintegration and partial secondary integration? We encounter them incessantly in daily life. If we feel hurt by somebody and react aggressively, we do not exhibit partial disintegration. However, if we try to analyze the circumstances in which we were hurt, if we try to understand the conditions which caused the other man to hurt us, we may refrain from reacting violently, we may find some reasons, which excuse his behavior. It will become much more understandable, and less hurting, possibly we may even experience feelings of friendliness toward the man and become aware of his difficulties and troubles. This*

> *attitude will eliminate the possibility of aggression and will generally increase our ability to understand people. It will allow for "openness" to difficulties experienced by other people and for a subtler, more sensitive, and farsighted behavior in the future.*
>
> *What took place in the above example was an inhibition of the usual "integrated" manner of response. In this way we broke down our mental structure of a low level and attained a partial integration at a higher level* (quotation marks in original text, Dąbrowski, 1970, p. 23).

In Dąbrowski's description of partial secondary integration, we can see emergence of the developmental dynamism of empathy. Empathy appears to spark the dynamism of self-control. The definition of developmental potential implies that empathy and self-control are the products of a multilevel view of the situation. Empathy and self-control, as dynamisms, are part of the autonomous forces component inherited with developmental potential. Furthermore, empathy is clearly an important aspect of emotional overexcitability, a critical factor in development. Since dynamisms are said to emerge from overexcitability, it can be said that its five forms work together to create a multilevel view of reality.

Dąbrowski provides a second example of partial secondary integration demonstrating the emergence of developmental dynamisms:

> *S., a high school student in grade nine, was given an unjustly low mark in a subject which he knew quite well. He experienced the apparent failure seriously which, most likely, was caused by a lack of attention on the part of the teacher or by the teacher's momentary negative attitude toward the boy, or by some other accidental circumstances. The pupil's first response was to refuse to go to school, to show aggressive feelings toward his teacher, to be rude to him. After some time, S. reconsidered the matter. He concluded that this kind of injustice is not necessarily a result of a conscious, deliberate act. Following the advice of his parents and the conclusions of his own deliberations,*

> he decided to refrain from any impulsive response and to do more homework. After a few weeks he received a good mark. The teacher thought the problem over and admitted that the low mark was not just. This inhibition, the internalization of this unpleasant fact, the ability to control a violent response, careful thought and reconsideration of the response led to a partial secondary integration on a higher level. (Dąbrowski, 1970, pp. 23-24)

S's initial negative responses to being treated unfairly were transformed as a result of S's reconsideration of the teacher's motivation and his reflection on parental advice. The example illustrates the emergence of self-control and autopsychotherapy. We can see that S's developmental dynamisms are part of his developmental potential.

Qualitatively different processes are inherent in the two examples. In the first example, reacting aggressively indicates a low level, perhaps a primary integrative response, which can be explained, if habitual, by insufficient developmental potential. In that case, the social cognitive theory of emotion adequately explains an aggressive response—appraisal of threat led to a defensive response. Since there is no reference to recall of the initial situation, no disintegrating dynamisms were triggered (see Chapter 6), and disintegrating dynamisms are necessary for growth. In contrast, inhibition of an aggressive response in the face of feeling hurt, accompanied by an attempt to understand the situation and the other person's behavior, suggests a higher level of development. Such responses display inner rather than external directedness, implying current activity of developmental dynamisms. Dąbrowski's explanation of the first example is, in fact, a description of how positive disintegration occurs at the micro level: mental structures at the lower level are broken, replaced by structures at a higher level.

In the second example, S's initial response is also understood by applying the social cognitive theory of emotion—S's response resulted from appraisal of his teacher's behavior as intentional, and therefore threatening to his personal well-being. Unlike the first example, S's initial threat appraisal was reconsidered after some time, implying recall of the original situation. Recall of emotionally charged social situations by individuals with ample developmental potential contributes to the rejection of primitive responses. Rejection of primitive responses by reflection or inhibition explains in general how developmental dynamisms emerge.

Examination of a common occurrence when people experience negative emotion may shed additional light on this matter. It is a truism that when we experience intense emotions, we cannot think clearly, regardless of our level of intelligence. In a sense, our cognitive capacity to think effectively is not accessible during the intense emotional experience. Our cognitive processing is almost completely engaged with the situation that we have appraised as threatening, and with the physiological feelings (e.g., increased heart rate, perspiration, etc.) that are part of experiencing such emotion. As emotional thoughts and feelings lessen and ultimately dissipate, our innate resources become accessible, enabling a dispassionate consideration of the stimulating social situation and our initial response to it. With the emotion dissipated, manifestations of developmental potential (developmental dynamisms, e.g., empathy, autopsychotherapy), are possible. With repeated practice, disintegrating dynamisms are no longer active because the lower forms of response evident in Dąbrowski's two examples are destroyed. Thoughtful consideration of social situations and our role in them occur as they happen, demonstrating a higher level of functioning characterized by the dynamisms empathy, self-control, and subject object in oneself.

It was noted earlier in this chapter that developmental dynamisms exist in nascent form—part of developmental potential—and that an initial overwhelming influence of biology and socialization block their emergence. Generally speaking, transcending the forces of biology and the social environment enables the emergence the developmental dynamisms. At the day-to-day level, individuals' experience of negative emotions, with its clouding of thinking, serves to block temporarily the appearance of developmental dynamisms for those with the prerequisite potential.

A final note: examples such as those provided by Dąbrowski, discussed earlier, illustrate that developmental dynamisms do not simply emerge once and become established. Empathy, for example, may occur sporadically, with lapses, for some time before it becomes entrenched, so to speak. Emergence is not to be confused with establishment. It likely takes years for individuals with a high level of developmental potential before some, if not all, developmental dynamisms become integrated into their daily lives.

PART III:
Dąbrowskian Constructs in Context

Chapter 8 Self
Chapter 9 Intelligence
Chapter 10 Hierarchy of Values
Chapter 11 Mental Health

Chapter 8
Self

With today's general public concern, if not obsession, with self-concept and the central place it holds in psychology, it is hard to fathom that there was a time when self-concept was practically unknown to parents, educators, counselors and psychologists. Surprisingly, attention was drawn to the importance of self-perception by scholars in the late nineteenth and early twentieth centuries, but the field of psychology itself largely ignored the construct until the mid- to late- twentieth century. The field of psychology may be forgiven for ignoring the works of the ideologically different scholars of sociology who drew attention to the importance of self-concept, such as Cooley (1964/1902) and G.H. Mead (1934). However, in retrospect it seems difficult to understand why psychology ignored the eminent psychologist William James, who focused on the importance of investigating individuals' perceptions of themselves beginning in the late nineteenth century (James, 1990/1890). In fact, it was about 60 years after James' work that there appears the first systematic study of self-concept from the field of psychology. Victor Raimy, in a study of counseling effectiveness (1948), reported that successful counseling enhanced a client's self-concept, while unsuccessful counseling did not. The question is: why did psychology ignore self-concept for such a long time? The answer lies in a paradigm which came to be known as behaviorism that afflicted psychology in the early part of the twentieth century. Pioneers in modern psychology were adamant that for psychology to be scientific, it had to adopt the methods of physics and chemistry, and tie itself to laboratories. In effect, the only valid domains of study were those which were observable; hence, behaviorism was the sole paradigm in psychology until the cognitive revolution in psychology which began in the 1950s and blossomed in the 1980s (Rosenberg, 1989). Carl Rogers (Rogers, 1961) and Abraham Maslow (1970) were instrumental in popularizing self-concept in psychology and in publications for general audiences. Today we can find thousands of studies and popular books regarding self-concept and its relative, self-esteem. Contrary to its contentious introduction, self-concept has become not only accepted, but also ubiquitous, in psychological studies and in public discourse.

Since the mid-twentieth century, there has been a significant burgeoning of research investigating self-concept with numerous variables and foci of interventions. It has become a mainstay of psychology and education. Self-concept is often represented as consisting of two facets: descriptive and evaluative. Self-concept is reserved for the descriptive facet while self-esteem represents the evaluative one. In general, though, self-concept is used as a synonym for self-esteem; that is, it is common practice to speak of positive or negative self-concept or self-esteem. For practitioners and the public, self-concept/self-esteem is an important correlate, if not a cause, of an individual's performance and mental state. For example, negative self-concept is associated with poor performance and with depression. Positive self-concept is associated with high performance and adjustment. Developing positive self-concepts in individuals and reducing negative self-concepts have become a central concern, if not a pre-occupation, of psychologists, educators, and parents. Nurturing positive self-concept has become part of the fabric of Western society, as evidenced in the goals of counselling, psychotherapy, teaching and parenting.

Absence of Self-Concept in the Theory of Positive Disintegration

While self-concept seems to be everywhere, it is not found in Dąbrowski's theory. There are countless occurrences of *self*, but no explicit reference to self-concept. A look at definitions explains the difference between self-concept and self. For the purposes of this discussion, I have adopted Morris Rosenberg's definition of self-concept who distinguishes between it and self-esteem. Rosenberg defines self-concept as "the totality of the individual's thoughts and feelings with reference to the self as object" (1989, p. 34). Rosenberg distinguishes self-concept and self-esteem by adding evaluative descriptors to his definition of self-concept. Self-esteem is a person's positive or negative attitude toward oneself and one's evaluation of own thoughts and feelings regarding oneself. Though self-concept and self-esteem do not appear in Dąbrowski's theory, Rosenberg's phrase "self as object" and self-evaluation are important concepts in Dąbrowski's theory.

Self as subject and *self as object* is a well-established dichotomy in the history of theorizing about self. For example, G. H. Mead (1934), used pronouns to distinguish between the two: *I*, refers to self as subject and *me*, to self as object. Self as subject represents agency, individuals as doers; self as object represents reflexivity, that is, an individual's reflection on *self* as an *object* like other objects in the environment. It is accepted that individuals experience self as both subject and object. Self as object is the substrate of self-concept. Occurrences of self in the theory of positive disintegration cannot be termed *self-concept*. However, the reflexivity of perceiving and evaluating self permeates the theory, as expressed explicitly in several dynamisms. All the disintegrating dynamisms, for example astonishment with self, are products of perceiving and evaluating self as object. Similarly, some developmental dynamisms are founded on self as object with self-awareness being an obvious example. Education of oneself, and autopsychotherapy also subsume self as object in mental processing. Subject-object in oneself not only illustrates the processing in question but also the simultaneous experiencing of self as subject and as object. Though self-concept *per se* is not found in Dąbrowski's theory, the process of reflecting on self as object permeates it.

The cognitive essence of self-concept—reflection on self as an object—is the one component of self-concept, as defined by Rosenberg, that is an integral part of the theory of positive disintegration. Self-evaluation aspect of self-esteem is also an important concept in the theory. From a Dąbrowskian point of view, it is the concern with negative self-concept/self-esteem, and veneration of their positive versions that make these concepts inconsistent with the theory. Absence of self-concept from the theory of positive disintegration is not an omission to be rectified but rather one to be understood as necessary given the nature of the theory. This understanding is based on an analysis of major theorizing about self-concept, contrasting it with key propositions and dynamisms of Dąbrowski's theory.

Self-Concept Formation

Reflected appraisal is by far the most influential theory of self-concept in both research and practice. It is likely the theory with which readers are most familiar, though they may not know its name. Reflected appraisal "refers to the processes by which people's self-views are influenced by their *perceptions* of how others view them" (Wallace & Tice, 2012, p. 124, italics added). According to this theory, what is important is not the actual views that others may have of us, but rather our inferences about others' views of us. Though only H. S. Sullivan (1953) uses the phrase, reflected appraisal is a theme consistent with several other pioneers who drew attention to self as object, including James, Cooley, G.H. Mead, and Rogers. Research support for reflected appraisal, using both correlational and experimental methods, is immense. "Overwhelming" is the word used by Wallace and Tice (2012, p. 124) to describe the volume of publications providing evidence for this theory of self-concept. Such support for a theory reminds us of the approach to *theory* in science. Theories are not proven but disproven. When attempts to disprove a theory fail, as in Newton's theory of gravity, it becomes a law. Given the overwhelming evidence in support of reflected appraisal, and the failure to disconfirm it after a multitude of attempts, we must conclude that it is not just a theory but a *law*. The law applies throughout the life span: perceptions of others' views of us influence self-concept from childhood to mature adulthood. Our perceptions determine the power and quality of self-concept. If we believe others' opinions of us are positive, the effect enhances our self-concept; belief that others' opinions of us are negative diminishes self-concept.

The theory of reflected appraisal not only identifies the influences on self-concept, but it also explains its creation. Self-concept is a social construct that is not present at birth but rather is created over time by individuals during their interactions with others. The main elements of reflected appraisal theory can be summarized as follows: self-concept emerges and develops through an individual's incorporation of feedback about themselves from significant others. *Emerges and develops* indicates that it is not present at birth and that it follows a developmental course. *Incorporation* (internalization) refers to an individual's cognitive processing of information. *Feedback about themselves* specifies the type of information being processed. The phrase *significant others* refers to persons whom individuals deem important to them. Normally these include parents, other family members, and teachers who are in positions to provide feedback to young people. In the reflected appraisal theory, self-concept is a mental construction produced by construal of self-referent feedback provided initially by caregivers, normally parents, and family members.

Self-concept has its origins in the socialization of children: childrearing provides endless opportunity for parents to provide children with feedback regarding them. In day-to-day interactions, parents convey their perceptions of their children through teaching appropriate behaviors, correcting inappropriate ones, and commenting on the personhood of their children. Parents' commentary to children is both descriptive and evaluative in nature. *Descriptive* feedback includes matters such as physical characteristics, ethnicity, religion, and gender. Such feedback leads to self-perceptions, for example, in my case: "I am a small boy who is Italian and Catholic". *Evaluative* feedback, as the term implies, includes parental assessments of appropriateness of behavior and valuation of their children. Evaluative feedback leads to self-perceptions such as "I am a good or bad boy." The two kinds of feedback contribute to the creation of two corresponding aspects of self-concept: descriptive, and evaluative. As noted earlier in this chapter, technically, *self-concept* itself refers to the descriptive component, while the evaluative part is known as *self-esteem*. Also recall that the distinction becomes moot since self-concept and self-esteem are often used interchangeably. *Positive* and *negative* are descriptors that are used with both self-concept and self-esteem. Parental interaction with children contributes to both aspects of self-concept. For better or worse, with respect to self-concept development, there can be no more important feedback than that of parents for young children. This is the primordial feedback, which is the raw material for self-concept development.

Feedback, in and of itself, is insufficient to trigger the emergence of self-concept. Children must internalize it, meaning that they must cognitively process the self-referent information. From a Piagetian perspective (see Chapter 2), children in the first stage of cognitive development, the sensorimotor stage (birth to two years) are not yet equipped to process incoming language-based commentary of any kind. In fact, <u>sensorimotor</u> experience is undifferentiated, with cognition linked exclusively to actions. In Piagetian theory, thought is equated with language (Piaget & Inhelder, 1969), suggesting that there is no thinking associated with the sensorimotor stage. Language acquisition begins between one and a half and two years of age, an important illustration of the symbolic function defining the pre-operational stage, two to seven years (Piaget, 1957). With language comes thought; however, its quality is rudimentary. Pre-operational thinking is characterized by egocentrism, a Piagetian concept that is different from words such as selfishness. Egocentrism is "a cognitive state in which the cognizer sees the world from one point of view—his own—but without knowledge of the existence of viewpoints or perspectives…" (Flavell, 1963, p. 60). It is cognitive self-centeredness, not to be equated with narcissism. I like Piaget and Inhelder's (1969) comment, repeated here: egocentrism is Freud's "narcissism without a Narcissus" (p. 22). Onset of language and thought, combined with parental feedback, trigger the emergence of self-concept. As language comprehension develops, children begin to perceive the self-referent comments parents provide. Parenting, independent of style, involves countless daily comments directed at children, ranging from teaching new behaviors, correcting inappropriate behaviors, describing developing personhood, and just plain chattering for fun. In other words, child-rearing is replete with parents' communication of their moment-to-moment assessment of their children's behaviors and attributes. That constitutes the feedback that children internalize—at a young age, parents' communications of their perceptions of children become children's perceptions of themselves. This is the beginning of self-concept.

Self-concept is a social construction; it is also a cognitive structure, affected by cognitive development. While young children can do very little to the incoming feedback from significant others, the situation changes as cognition matures, especially with the acquisition of abstract reasoning, part of Piaget's formal operations stage associated with early adolescence. During the early years, the reflected appraisal approach explains that children's self-perceptions mirror significant others' perceptions of them and stipulates who these significant others are. Acquisition of abstract reasoning enables individuals to scrutinize both the quality of feedback and who is in fact important to them. Before reaching early adolescence, children have little choice but to unconsciously accept unvarnished commentary directed at them by parents, older siblings, and by parent surrogates such as teachers. On the other hand, adolescents and adults with abstract reasoning ability can question the accuracy of feedback and decide whether the person who the source of the feedback is important to them. With mature cognition, there is also the capacity for self-awareness, which one can use to assess the validity of others' perceptions of oneself. Through self-observation an individual can have direct influence on self-concept. Having said that, perceptions of individuals by others continue in importance throughout life: others' perceptions may be dismissed but not necessarily ignored.

While the life-long feedback received is both descriptive and evaluative, it is not surprising that the evaluative type is more significant to individuals. Whether it is called self-esteem or self-concept, the consolidation of evaluative feedback over time has strong emotional and motivational power in an individual's daily living. Of course, it is positive self-esteem that is prized; low self-esteem requires enhancement. That positive self-esteem is associated with successful performance in many, if not all, aspects of life is part of the fabric of western culture.

Conclusions regarding self-concept. As I said earlier, the primary interest in reflected appraisal theory lies in its explanation of how self-concept is created. However, internalizing feedback from others is not restricted to young children. The process of reflected appraisal is evident in life beyond childhood. Our understanding of others' perceptions of us, communicated verbally and nonverbally, continues to affect us throughout life. As in childhood, it is the evaluative feedback that is most germane. However, unlike children, older individuals can consider the sources of feedback; they can identify which people encountered in social interactions are important and which are not. For example, not all teachers are important to adolescents; therefore, not all teachers' perceptions of students have equal impact on their self-concepts. Similarly, when faced with self-referent feedback from others in the social environment, adults are able to consider the source of the remarks, and so the feedback does not necessarily have an impact on self-concept. While acceptance of perceptions becomes more of a choice, older individuals are nonetheless generally affected by others' perceptions, especially from those that they deem important.

My personal and professional experience supports the idea that the initial self-concept which emerged during the early years, based on perceptions communicated by parents and other important people, persist into adulthood. There is little doubt that parents are the most influential people in our lives. Their perceptions of us communicated during childhood are crystalized into our self-concept, which seems to remain somewhat stable throughout life. With mature mental capacities, we can alter our self-concepts, though it must be emphasized that once formed in our early years of life, self-concept is resistant to change.

It appears that the law of reflected appraisal is endemic in human beings. Most if not all individuals develop a self-concept. Due to its development, we become sensitive to the descriptive and evaluative feedback we receive from others. Unless we try to disentangle ourselves from the influence of other people's responses to us, especially from the feedback we received during our early years, we are destined to maintain a variation of the original, rudimentary self-concept. In addition, without such distancing of ourselves from our initial self-concept, we are likely to remain influenced by what we believe others think of us.

In the theory of positive disintegration, developmental potential enables individuals to rise above their original, socially constructed self-concept.

The Absence of Self-Concept in Dąbrowski's Theory Explained

Self-concept is the offspring of an individual's internalization of perceptions garnered from the social environment. Developmental potential places individuals on a path of advanced development, indicating transcendence of the demands of the social environment. Viewing the analysis of self-concept development through a Dąbrowskian lens should alert readers to the explanation why self-concept cannot be part of what the theory considers advanced development. Recall that Dąbrowski identifies three factors of development: biology, first factor; social environment, second factor; autonomous forces, third factor. If only the first two factors are present, we have what he would call normal development. It is obvious that self-concept, as conceived through the theory of reflected appraisal, is created almost entirely by the operation of the second factor of development. Self-concept is not only influenced by our interactions with significant others (social environment); it is created by them. Furthermore, internalizing of others' perceptions implies internalizing societal values which are implicitly and explicitly communicated in self-referent feedback. Development requires transcendence of the effects of the first and second factors, driven by the actions of the third factor. Self-concept, including positive self-concept, is not an indicator of advanced development.

Conceptually, striving for positive self-concept/self-esteem has no place in the theory of positive disintegration. Both the disintegrating dynamisms of spontaneous multilevel disintegration (Level III) and the developmental dynamisms of organized multilevel disintegration (Level IV) argue against the relevance of positive self-concept. Disintegrating dynamisms, in self-concept terms, describe low self-esteem conditions. Feelings of guilt, shame and dissatisfaction with self are not only necessary for positive disintegration, but they also define it. Inner conflict, the hallmark of Level III, has the appearance of a chronic low self-esteem condition. However, in Dąbrowski's theory, the negative feelings about self—disintegrating dynamisms—are not to be confused with low self- esteem, which results from internalizing other people's negative perceptions. Instead, the negative feelings are the product of awareness of the discrepancy between one's thoughts and behaviors, and one's emerging values.

Developmental dynamisms do not involve positive self-concept or self-esteem. Level IV dynamisms do not describe people who are feeling good about themselves based on internalizing other people's positive perceptions, nor is positive self-evaluation part of developmental dynamisms. Developmental dynamisms, in fact, explicitly contradict the experience of positive self-concept. A central dynamism of Level IV, autonomy, specifically refers to the achievement of transcending the effects of the social environment. Dynamisms that include self, such as self-control and self-awareness, refer to controlling one's impulses and to understanding oneself, respectively. Therefore, positive self-concept/self-esteem, has no place, no meaning in the theory of positive disintegration. Of all the terms related to self, such as self-concept, self-esteem, self-evaluation, and self-acceptance that appear in the literature, *self-acceptance* is likely the most apt term to describe self-related experience in the theory of positive disintegration.

While self-concept has no place in Dąbrowski's theory, *self* does. Disintegrating and developmental dynamisms can be categorized as expressing self as object or self as subject. Disintegrating dynamisms such as astonishment, guilt, shame, and dissatisfaction, for example, manifest self as object. Individuals cannot experience such self-referent emotions without becoming objects of their own awareness. Similarly, some developmental dynamisms, such as self-awareness, education of oneself and autopsychotherapy imply an ongoing perception of oneself as object. On the other hand, developmental dynamisms of autonomy, authentism, responsibility, and empathy manifest self as subject. As noted earlier, subject-object in oneself manifests the actions of both selves. The dialogue that occurs between self as object and self as subject maintains advanced development.

Conclusion

My thinking about reflected appraisal, self-concept, and dynamisms over the years led me to wonder which, if any, of the numerous terms for *self* would be appropriate for use in the theory of positive disintegration. Self-acceptance, as noted above, appeared promising. Though advanced development is characterized by self-acceptance, I believe the phrase does not capture the essential nature of self at the highest levels of development. No typical self-term seemed appropriate. After much deliberation, I decided upon *autonomous self*. Autonomy, a developmental dynamism of Level IV/V, formed by the actions of the third factor and inner psychic transformation, inspired my choice. With its meaning rooted in the high-level dynamism, *autonomous* is a perfect descriptor for the quality of self in advanced development in the theory of positive disintegration. Dąbrowski (1970) described autonomy as a dynamism of inner freedom enabling individuals to create their true selves, and to become self-determining agents of their development—a stark contrast to the creation of self-concept!

Autonomous self provides a different way to describe development in the theory of positive disintegration. My usual succinct description of development is that it is the progression from lower forms of thinking and behaving to higher forms. Contrasting self-concept, conceived theoretically using the reflected appraisal approach, with Dąbrowski's *self* provides a new concise description: advanced development is a progression from self-concept to autonomous self. Self-concept is meaningful in normal development, autonomous self, in advanced development.

CHAPTER 9
Intelligence

With the preponderance of attention given to emotions and values in academic and popular writings on the theory of positive disintegration, it may come as a surprise to some readers that Dąbrowski had a great deal to say about the construct of *intelligence*. There are countless occurrences of the term in his writings, as well as references to the related concept, cognitive development, which he termed *mental growth* (Dąbrowski, 1970). Dąbrowski's propositions regarding the construct, taken together, constitute an implicit theory of intelligence. In this chapter, I discuss Dąbrowski's implicit theory and contrast it with established theories of intelligence. Of the numerous psychological theories available, I have selected those of three historical theorists who have had significant influence which persists to present day: Spearman (1904), R.B. Cattell (1943) and Wechsler (1944). By contrasting what I term Dąbrowski's implicit theory with the latter theories, the aim is to capture the fullness of his thinking on intelligence.

*I*ntelligence: Easy to See; Hard to Define

It is safe to say that people, in general, do not know what intelligence is, but they "know it when they see it". People who think about such things may believe that, while they do not know what it is, presumably scholars in the field of psychology do know. In a way that is correct, because numerous scholars in the history of psychology have *believed* that they know. Such scholars spent a significant part of their careers arriving at a definition of intelligence, with the remainder of their working lives devoted to convincing other scholars and researchers that their conceptions were correct. From the dawn of modern psychology in the late 19th century to the beginning of the 21st century, Sattler (2001) identified 18 definitions of intelligence. Recently, Wasserman (2018) listed some 30 definitions, including many definitions proposed by lesser-known names in psychology, but scholars, nonetheless. Conceptions of intelligence in the history of psychology are generally associated with two groups of individuals: those concerned with construction of intelligence tests, and others interested in statistical analyses of test results, leading to the production of their theories.

Notable among individuals interested in test construction are Francis Galton, Alfred Binet, Lewis Terman and David Wechsler, each with his own conception of intelligence underlying the tests. Galton's test assessed individuals' physical properties with particular focus on sensory acuity, which he believed formed the substrate of intelligence, though not intelligence itself (Wasserman, 2018). Binet, with Theodore Simon, produced the first practical intelligence test (Sattler, 2001), introducing the concept of *mental level*. In 1912, William Stern proposed dividing the mental level, which he called *mental age*, by chronological age, thereby calculating an *intelligence quotient* (Thorndike, 1997). Thus, was born the IQ that is prominent in professional and public discourse to this very day. Terman (1916) revised the Binet-Simon test for use in the US. Wechsler developed intelligence tests that proved over time to be the most popular, as indicated by their wide usage. Indeed, Wechsler's tests are the most widely used of all psychological tests. A variety of conceptions of intelligence underlie the intelligence tests created by these test developers.

Notable among individuals who used statistical analyses of tests to infer their conceptions of intelligence include Spearman, Thurstone and R.B. Cattell. Spearman arrived at his two-factor theory of intelligence, the famous *g* (denoting general intelligence) and lesser-known *s* (denoting specific mental abilities), based on the analysis of correlations (factor analysis) among subscales of intelligence tests. Using an approach like Spearman's, Thurstone developed his multidimensional theory, and R.B. Cattell, with Horn, developed his fluid and crystallized theory. In addition to the practitioners and scholars mentioned above, numerous other conceptions of intelligence are evident in the annals of psychology. Among the more well-known recent theorists are Gardner and Sternberg. Gardner proposed his version of multiple intelligences while Sternberg developed a triarchic theory of intelligence. Gardner and Sternberg are the latest contributors to the divergence of definitions.

The lack of consensus regarding a definition of intelligence has been considered problematic; after all, intelligence is likely the most-researched construct in psychology, and as such, it seems reasonable to expect a convergence of definitions. Attempts to remedy the divergence began a hundred years ago (Pinter, 1921) and have been repeated more recently by Sternberg and Detterman (1986). Regrettably, attempts to reach agreement on a common definition have been unsuccessful. As Wasserman (2018) lamented: "The failure to arrive at a consensus on defining *intelligence* after a century of research constitutes one of the most surprising loose threads in the history of psychology" (p. 35).

My view on the enduring lack of unanimity on defining intelligence differs; multiple conceptions of intelligence suggest to me that no one really knows what intelligence is. Yet, we know it when we see it. Actually, the reason why there are so many definitions is because we *cannot see* intelligence. If we could see it in the material environment, in this case in the human organism, we could arrive relatively quickly at a consensus on its distinguishing characteristics. We do not have a plethora of definitions for objects that we *can* see regarding the human organism, such as heart, lungs, and brain. Similarly, there is general agreement on terminology for objects in the physical environment, such as, tree, table, lake, and meadow. Though there are varying versions of objects, we agree on their defining properties—there are many varieties of trees, but we generally recognize a tree when we see it. Such is not the case with psychological terms. In the field of psychology numerous definitions are not unique to the construct of intelligence. Without listing the entire lexicon of psychology, suffice it to say that, with few exceptions, there is no consensus on psychological terminology. Notable exceptions include physiological terms such as those delineating parts of the brain (e.g., the cortex) and diagnostic categories of disorders (e.g., ADHD, a psychiatric term adopted by psychology).

Influential Conceptions of Intelligence

Of the numerous original historical conceptions of intelligence, the influence of three proponents continues in present day psychological research and practice. Though Gardner's theory of multiple intelligences and Sternberg's triarchic theory are popular in some quarters, it is the works of Spearman, Wechsler, and Cattell that are by far the most influential conceptions of intelligence. Spearman's general intelligence theory, which dominated the field until the 1930s, continues to inspire research in present day psychology (e.g., Warne & Bummingham, 2019). The core of Spearman's conception is that intelligence consists of a general factor (g) with one or more specific mental abilities (s). According to Sattler (2001): "Spearman thought of the g factor as general mental energy with complicated mental activities containing the greatest amount of g." Sattler goes on to say: [T]he g factor is an index of general mental ability or intelligence…." (p.138). Though Spearman's conception is termed two factors, his view of intelligence itself is unitary.

The visibility of Spearman's ideas in research is outweighed by the invisibility of his influence: his view of general intelligence has become part of the fabric of the psychology of intelligence. Similar to Freud's *ego* and Rogers' *empathy*, which are used in general and academic discourse without reference to the original authors who popularized the terms, Spearman's name is no longer associated with *general intelligence*, except of course, when researchers are investigating g.

Wechsler's original definition of intelligence is operationalized in the tests that he created. Wechsler's conception of intelligence is as follows:

> *Intelligence is the aggregate or [and] global capacity of the individual to behave purposefully, to think rationally and to deal effectively with his [or her] environment. It is global because it characterizes the individual's behavior as a whole; it is an aggregate because it is composed of elements or abilities which, though not entirely independent,*

are qualitatively differentiable. By measurement of these abilities, we ultimately evaluate intelligence. (Wechsler, 1944, p. 3; italics in original; words added)

The definition is reflected in the structure of Wechsler tests, such as the Wechsler Intelligence Scale for Children, Fifth Edition (WISC V), that provides an overall assessment of general cognitive ability (Full Scale IQ) and index scores of intellectual functioning in verbal comprehension, visual-spatial, fluid reasoning, working memory and processing speed (Kaufman, Raiford, & Coalson, 2016). I initially recognized aspects of both Spearman's and Piaget's conceptions of intelligence in the definition. *Aggregate or global capacity* is Spearman's general factor of intelligence. Wechsler might disagree with his definition being associated with Spearman's perspective, inasmuch as Wechsler (1944) suggests an ambivalent attitude toward Spearman. On the one hand he praises Spearman: "Professor Spearman's generalized proof of the two-factor theory of human abilities constitutes one of the great discoveries of psychology" (p.6). On the other hand, he is critical about the famous g.

> *Just what "g" is psychologically and to what extent it may be identified with general intelligence, are still matters of speculation and dispute… [T]he present author [Wechsler] is far from being in full agreement with Professor Spearman's concept of general intelligence or even with his views regarding the best mode of measuring it, but regarding the demonstration of the existence of "g" as a common factor, there seems to be no possibility of doubt. Psychometrics, without it, loses its basic prop* (p. 7-8).

At times, Wechsler seems to trivialize Spearman's pronouncements about general intelligence. For example:

> *As is often the case in science, the proof of the two-factor theory, in addition to being a discovery, was also an explicit formulation of an hypothesis which workers in the field had unknowingly been assuming for some time. The fact is, that from the day psychologists began to use a series of*

tests for measuring intelligence, they necessarily assumed the existence of a general or common factor. (p. 6)

Regarding the other component of Wechsler's definition—*to deal effectively with his environment*—I assumed that it reflected Piaget's influence on Wechsler; however, it was Binet who influenced that part of Wechsler's definition. Wasserman (2018) noted that Wechsler himself acknowledged Binet as the source:

According to Wechsler (Wechsler et al, 1975), this definition also subsumes Binet's emphasis on adaptation. The phrase "to deal effectively with his environment" recapitulates Binet's (1911/1916) observation that "intelligence marks itself by the best possible adaptation of the individual to his environment" (p. 301), as well as the use of adaptation in the definition of intelligence by others. (p. 32).

As an aside, some of the basic Piagetian concepts were also foreshadowed by Binet. Siegler (1992) noted that Binet's work in cognition includes some foundational concepts associated with Piaget's theory. These include among other ideas "that the purpose of cognitive development is adaptation to the physical and social worlds" (Siegler, p. 183). And so, according to Wechsler intelligence is an aggregate of abilities and is manifested in one's adaptation to social and physical environments.

Cattell's Fluid and Crystallized Intelligences

While Wechsler had his issues with Spearman, general intelligence is at the core of his definition and, ironically, the total IQ score of the Wechsler tests has continued to be considered an excellent estimate of **g**. In contrast, Cattell's original two factor conception of intelligence (Cattell, 1943) rejected Spearman's definition outright. Cattell was not alone in questioning Spearman's notion that intelligence is unitary. In the 1930s, Spearman's domination of the field had begun to wane and the view that intelligence is unitary began to be replaced by other conceptions of intelligence. For example, Thurstone (1938) proposed a multifactor theory composed of seven primary factors in contrast to Spearman's single factor, **g.** That is, Thurstone and others proposed that intelligence is multiple not unitary. Cattell (1971) describes his own questioning of Spearman's influence as he succinctly explains the origin of his own theorizing:

> *It [g] had become the scientists' [scholars of intelligence] touchstone to which all debated practical issues in interpreting and using intelligence tests and the I.Q. were referred. However, in the mid-thirties some half-dozen different lines of evidence converged in the present writer's [Cattell's] thinking to suggest the disturbing idea that g might be two general factors instead of one! The notion was disturbing to the writer personally because of his association and his great regard for Spearman and his work.* (pp. 74-75; bracketed remarks added).

Cattell, rejecting the idea of a single general factor, proposed his own unique version of multiple intelligences. The original theory (Cattell, 1943) consisted of two general factors: general fluid intelligence (Gf) and general crystalized intelligence (Gc). Gf is the more powerful factor and consists of the purely physiological influences of heredity and maturity of neural development (Eno, 1978), affecting performance on all tasks that require perception of novel relationships (Martinez, 2019). Gc consists of skills and habits of thinking, which were "originally learned through the action of fluid intelligence but which no longer requires them for successful operation" (Eno, 1978, p. 817). A central difference between Gf and Gc can be summarized succinctly by paraphrasing Blanch (2015): Gf is driven by biology; Gc by culture.

Certain cognitive abilities are associated with each of Cattell's general intelligences. For example, Schneider & McGrew (2018) noted that Gf includes "the use of deliberate and controlled procedures (often requiring focused attention) to solve novel, 'on-the-spot' problems that cannot be solved by using previously learned habits, schemas, and scripts" (p. 93). They note that Gc includes "the ability to comprehend and communicate culturally valued knowledge…[and] the depth and breadth of both declarative and procedural knowledge, and skills such as language, words, and general knowledge developed through experience, learning, and acculturation" (p. 114). Sun,

Nancekivell, Gelman, and Shah (2021) differentiated the cognitive activities of Gf and Gc as follows:

> *Fluid intelligence refers to how an individual solves novel reasoning problems by identifying abstract patterns and relations and using inductive and deductive logic. In contrast, crystallized intelligence consists of an individual's knowledge and skills and their ability to apply them in different domains.* (p. 816)

To review, Gf is biologically based, heritable, general cognitive ability, enabling an individual's understanding of and solving of novel problems and demands. In contrast, Gc is the repository of culturally acquired knowledge, primarily the product of Gf in combination with other personality traits such as motivation (Martinez, 2019). Gc is a repository of accrued knowledge learned through an individual's practice of Gf as they participate in a particular culture. Novel problems requiring abstract reasoning require Gf. Scientific and technological advances, such as advances in understanding of subatomic particles and the creation of computers, require high levels of Gf. Students of physics and information technologies also need Gf when they first encounter concepts in their respective fields, though not as much as was required by the innovators. Once learned, students can apply the concepts using Cattell's Gc. Since not all of us have the intelligence to be "rocket scientists" or to be students of physics or computer science, it stands to reason that individuals manifest different levels of Gf. Because it is a heritable characteristic, individuals are endowed with various levels of Gf.

The significant difference between Gf and Gc is described vividly by Cattell, in a letter written in the 1940s. In it he notes metaphorically that Gf is the "live" intelligence compared to Gc. "[T]he level of 'crystallized abilities [which] has been largely determined by the original level of the all-round 'fluid' ability is thus the *dead coral formation* revealing the limits of the original living process" (cited in Brown, 2016, p. 5).

A comment is in order regarding my interpretation of the Gf-Gc relationship. Gc knowledge is not always the product of Gf.

Given the biological basis of Gf, with its defining quality of abstract reasoning, Gc is active before Gf in the early years of life. This is supported by the fact that, physiologically, Gf is defined in terms of neuronal maturity; psychologically, it is defined by the acquisition of abstract reasoning. Physiologically, neuronal maturation seems to be attained in young adulthood according to research on brain development. Psychologically, abstract reasoning should occur in adolescence, with the attainment of the formal operation stage of cognitive development. Until then, Gc intelligence itself is responsible for environmental learning. Children learn a great deal due to the cultural requirement to teach children the demands of a society in which they are born. Through socialization practices, children learn appropriate behavior, norms, and values, through the intervention of parents and educators. Once learned, the knowledge gained can be generalized to other domains; for example, acceptable behavior learned at home is applied in school settings. Gc is intelligence in its own right, responsible for learning new information and applying it in other domains. An important consideration when distinguishing Gc from Gf is that socialization practices have their origin in the environment: parents and teachers explain what is appropriate; children do not need to discover what is appropriate behavior or an acceptable norm. Socialization requires a type of intelligence that enables children to understand what, for example, parents are communicating: Gc. While the demands of socialization are novel for children when first encountered, there is no need for children's cognitive ability to discover them.

About 80 years after the earliest publication in which the two intelligences were introduced (Cattell, 1943), research interest in Gf and Gc persists (e.g., Conte et al., 2020; Kaya et al, 2015; Schroeder et al., 2016; Thorsen et al., 2014). This is the case despite the recent embedding of Cattell's theory into the multidimensional Cattell-Horn-Carroll theory of intelligence (Schneider & McGrew, 2018). Cattell's original two intelligences themselves continue to inspire research.

Wechsler's concept of intelligence is, in effect, Spearman's general factor intelligence, measured by an aggregate of abilities. Cattell's definition, on the other hand, differs significantly from that of

Spearman. Fluid intelligence is biologically based, responsible for handling novel situations; crystallized intelligence is the product of fluid intelligence. In a sense, Cattell's crystallized intelligence elevates Wechsler's *adaptation* component to a separate cognitive ability that forms a repository of knowledge acquired by living in a culture. These are the conceptions of intelligence to which Dąbrowski's theorizing will be compared.

Uncovering Dąbrowski's Implicit Theory of Intelligence

I find it interesting that intelligence is one of the few—if not the only— mainstream psychological constructs that Dąbrowski does not explicitly reframe. *Development, maladjustment,* and *disintegration* are all constructs that he redefined, such that their definitions are opposites of their meaning in psychology. Not only is intelligence not reframed in the theory, but it is also not defined. It may be that Dąbrowski believed, consciously or unconsciously, that there was no need to define it, in that the definition he adopted was obvious from the contexts in which he used it. That explanation seems plausible: he used Wechsler's tests in his clinical work (Tillier, 2018) and in his research: "For the purpose of our research intelligence was evaluated using the Wechsler Adult Intelligence Scale" (Dąbrowski, 1996, p.182). It seems reasonable to assume, then, that when he uses *intelligence*, it is Wechsler's definition. In addition, in the theory of positive disintegration there are references to low, average, and high levels of intelligence. References to such individual differences are reflective of intelligence as measured by the Wechsler tests measuring children's and adults' intelligence. The definition of intelligence, then, in the theory of positive disintegration, is readily inferred. Dąbrowski's intelligence may be described as *general intellectual capacity*, manifested in the level of adaptation to the environment. Though Wechsler does not include individual differences in his conception of intelligence—apparently none of the theorists do—it is obvious in his approach to measuring intelligence.

Understanding Dąbrowski's *intellectual overexcitability*, in contrast to *intelligence*, requires no inference. This form of overexcitability is amply defined. Dąbrowski (1996) states that it is a form of overexcitability that is "manifested as a drive to ask probing questions, avidity for knowledge, theoretical thinking, reverence for logic, preoccupation with theoretical problems, etc." (p. 72). This form of overexcitability operates in "planning and solving problems" (1996, p.181).

I suggest that general intellectual capacity (Wechsler's intelligence) and intellectual overexcitability, taken together comprise Dąbrowski's conception of intelligence. In the parlance of the field of intelligence, Dąbrowski's is a *two intelligences* theory. Like Cattell's distinction between crystallized and fluid intelligence, Dąbrowski distinguishes between general intellectual capacity and intellectual overexcitability. In several places in his books, Dąbrowski makes it clear that intelligence (general intellectual capacity) and intellectual overexcitability are distinct. For example, Dąbrowski (1996) writes:

> *Here caution: intellectual overexcitability should not be confused with intellectual functioning and intelligence. Under the term intellectual overexcitability we put those forms of enhanced reactivity which are expressed in logical and causal cognition focused on finding answers to probing questions* (p.182).

Dąbrowski's two intelligences, like Cattell's fluid and crystallized forms, are distinct but related. In the case of Cattellian intelligence, the relationship is stipulated: crystallized intelligence is the product of fluid intelligence. The relationship between intellectual overexcitability and intellectual capacity seems obvious. Intellectual overexcitability subsumes a high level of intelligence; the opposite is not true: intelligence does not subsume the overexcitability. Intellectual capacity, as intelligence, has meaning in the context of Wechsler's theorizing, where it is an isolated construct. It is "free standing", not part of an overall theory. Intellectual overexcitability is part of the larger Dąbrowskian factor of developmental potential, as one of five forms of overexcitability. Intellectual overexcitability is required, along with the other forms, for advanced development; intelligence, even at the high level, is not. Dąbrowski makes this point clear by the proposition that a high level of intelligence is necessary but not sufficient for advanced development. A high level of intelligence separate from intellectual overexcitability may contribute to what Dąbrowski called one-sided development. In its positive form, this type of development is manifested by great success in one's field of endeavor and is characterized by a lack of personal growth. In its negative form, it is evident in current and historical despots and certain criminals.

An additional proposition in Dąbrowski's implicit theory of intelligence is that the role of intelligence is a function of a level of development. In primary integration: "Intelligence neither controls nor transforms basic drives; it serves the ends determined by primitive drives" (Dąbrowski, 1996, p. 18). However, with the influence of positive disintegration, during spontaneous and organized multilevel disintegration, intelligence changes from "a blind instrument in the service of impulses to a major force helping the individual to seize life deeply, wholly and objectively" (Dąbrowski, 1964, p. 67). And so, it can be concluded that intelligence is subservient—a tool or instrument— to the prevailing factors in a level of development. In Level I, intelligence is a tool of drives, instincts and demands of society. In Levels III and IV, intelligence is no longer subservient to the demands of biology and society, but rather, it becomes a major force contributing to an individual's development.

A question arises: is it the *changing role* of intelligence in the various levels, or is it the absence or presence of *intellectual overexcitability*? To answer the question, I assume that it is a high level of intelligence that is involved in its changing role. One possibility is that in the case of primary integration, the function of intelligence is fixed, subservient to the demands of that level. In the case of higher levels of development, it may be that the apparent change in intelligence is an illusion—it may simply be the emergence of intellectual overexcitability. However, intellectual overexcitability along with high intelligence are noticeable at a young age. One may hypothesize that it takes a while for intellectual overexcitability to "blossom", while high intelligence is seen sooner in children's cleverness. Unfortunately, such an explanation would be inconsistent with Dąbrowski's view that all forms of overexcitability may be evident in children as young as one or two years of age.

An answer to the question of changing role of intelligence may be inferred by examining Dąbrowski's description of the function of intellectual overexcitability in the levels of development; in all levels there are references to intelligence (Dąbrowski, 1996). At Level I, Dąbrowski uses the analogy of a computer to describe the main activity of intellectual overexcitability. It is manifested in the manipulation of data and other information. In his depiction of the overexcitability in primary integration, he refers to intelligence as follows: "Intelligence rather than intellectual overexcitability serves as an instrument subservient to the dictates of primitive drives" (Dąbrowski, 1996, p. 78). At Level II, the overexcitability is manifested in impressive and even brilliant acquisition of knowledge. Consistent with the dynamics of the unilevel disintegration phase, learning is unsystematic, lacking a clear valuing of the process of knowledge acquisition. Level II dynamisms (ambivalence and ambitendencies) signal the dislodging of the link between intelligence and primitive drives. In the first two levels, intellectual overexcitability tends to operate in isolation of the other forms. It is at Level III that its contribution to development comes to light. Inner conflict and the dynamisms are intensified by intellectual overexcitability. Awareness of the world and self are increased by this overexcitability. Understanding human experience is added to a hunger for learning and understanding phenomena. Level III also notes a change in its operating in isolation from other forms, though its encounters with the emotional form leads to instances of both conflict and cooperation. There is also development of what Dąbrowski termed "intuitive intelligence" (p. 78). At Level IV and beyond, all five forms of overexcitability work in unison, producing highly creative intelligence. Intellectual interests are described as extensive, universal, and multilevel. In the theory of positive disintegration, not only the function of intelligence changes with development but also that of intellectual overexcitability.

Dąbrowski's explanation that both intelligence and intellectual overexcitability are transformed by positive disintegration fits well with the idea of two intelligences. One possibility is that intelligence is employed in meeting the demands of daily living in the social environment, while intellectual overexcitability enriches daily living.

In a way Dąbrowski's two intelligences are analogous to Cattell's fluid and crystallized intelligence. Fluid intelligence is activated by the demands of novel situation and challenges; crystallized intelligence works with accumulated knowledge. Similarly, intellectual overexcitability provides impetus for logical reasoning and theoretical matters; intelligence is concerned with using learned cognitive abilities to handle daily life. Intellectual overexcitability is not needed to efficiently handle routines of daily living; one possibility is that the overexcitability overrides the role of intelligence. Individuals who are overly excitable intellectually may go without food or sleep when they are involved in solving a highly theoretical challenge. At some point, such individuals will have to resort to their intelligence to get food and some sleep. With development, intelligence is harnessed to deal with handling daily living in a sensitive, ethical manner; intellectual overexcitability combines with other forms of overexcitability to enhance personal growth.

Concerning the analogy between Dąbrowski's and Cattell's two intelligences: while there is some similarity between the two, there are qualitative differences. Dąbrowski's intelligence, presumed to be Weschler's definition, and general crystalized intelligence (Gc) share the common feature of acquired knowledge. Gc refers to knowledge acquired by living in a culture (e.g., child rearing practices, attending school, etc.). Intelligence as Wechsler's general intellectual capacity includes the notion of adaptation to the social environment. Adaptation requires learning the expectations of a culture, like Gc. On the other hand, there is little overlap between general fluid intelligence (Gf) and intellectual overexcitability. Both Gf and intellectual overexcitability are needed for problem-solving in common. However, they are qualitatively different in that Gf is reactive to the environment, in effect reflecting a stimulus-response mode. Intellectual overexcitability is not simply reactive but also additive. In other words, fluid intelligence responds effectively to novel problems encountered in the environment; whereas intellectual overexcitability, in addition to responding to problems, also creates or invents them. It seems reasonable to propose that intellectual overexcitability subsumes Cattell's fluid intelligence as well as Wechsler's intelligence.

Conclusion

Dąbrowski's name does not appear in the annals of the history of intelligence in psychology, though he wrote a great deal on the subject. A perusal of his writings reveals examination of intelligence and intellectual overexcitability—a special form of intelligence—and their relationship. Propositions regarding the relevance of his two intelligences and levels of human development can be extracted from his commentary. Taken together the latter elements form a coherent whole—Dąbrowski's implicit theory of intelligence. When contrasted with established conceptions of intelligence Dąbrowski's conception aligns structurally with Cattell's two intelligences. Conceptually, though, there are significant differences. Dąbrowski's implicit theory subsumes both fluid and crystallized intelligences. Another difference is that Dąbrowski's pronouncements regarding intelligence, unlike Cattell's formulation, amount to a *theory*, not a mere conception, of intelligence.

Theory of intelligence is not a phrase that comes to mind when thinking of Dąbrowski's positive disintegration. Nonetheless, his explanation of the movement from primitive to advanced development can be conceptualized as a transformation of intellectual functioning. This is made clear in its emphasis on mental growth. Constructing his implicit theory of intelligence aims to remind us that, when all is said and done, positive disintegration is produced by, and dramatically changes, our *thinking*.

Chapter 10
Hierarchy of Values

Unless students of Dąbrowski's theory are also students of social psychology, their first encounter with *hierarchy of values* likely occurs in learning about the theory of positive disintegration. As it turns out, there is a body of literature in psychology that has accrued since the 1970s on values, and their arrangement in systems or hierarchies. While the topic of values has been the preoccupation of philosophers for centuries, it was the work of Rokeach (1968, 1973) that sparked interest for psychological research on the topic. Undoubtedly, the dramatic arousal of interest in research about values and hierarchy of values was the result of Rokeach's creating an operational definition for his conceptualizations. In order to test his theorizing, he produced the Rokeach Value Survey (Rokeach, 1973). The theory has significantly influenced the study of values in social psychology. Rokeach's continuing influence can be seen in both theory (e.g., see Schwartz (1992, 2012) and research [e.g., Finlay et al (2015); Aavik & Dobewall (2017)]. Rokeach's theory of human values is a comprehensive, coherent conceptualization of values and their organization into a hierarchy.

Though "hierarchy of values" is not unique to the theory of positive disintegration, Dąbrowski reframes its meaning and associates it with advanced development itself, as he did with other established psychological constructs. A comparison of Dąbrowski's theorizing with that of Rokeach demonstrates Dąbrowski's unique approach to hierarchy of values.

Rokeach's Theory of Human Values

Milton Rokeach's first formal presentation of his theory of human values was likely his presidential address to the Society for the Psychological Study of Social Issues of the American Psychological Association, September 2, 1967, later published in the Journal of Social Issues (Rokeach, 1968). His address was an argument for elevating values to a prominent position in social psychology. At the time, social psychology was preoccupied with the concept of attitudes. Essentially, Rokeach wanted *values* to replace the position held by attitudes. In 1968, he wrote:

> *It is now exactly half a century since Thomas and Znaniecki (1918) first proposed that the study of social attitudes should be the central problem of social psychology. In the intervening years the attitude concept has indeed occupied a dominant place in theory and research.... Now, half a century later, the time is perhaps ripe to re-open the question as to whether the attitude concept should continue to occupy the central position it has enjoyed for so long* (p. 14).

It is beyond the scope of this chapter to determine whether the concept of values is preeminent in social psychology today. Suffice it to say that database searches reveal numerous citations to values and Rokeach's approach to them. It seems that Rokeach single handedly raised values to an eminent, if not preeminent, place in social psychology. Rokeach created a theory of values complete with assumptions, definitions, propositions, and a device for assessing his conceptualizations.

Assumptions

Rokeach (1973) identified five assumptions that underlie his theory of human values:

> *(1) the total number of values that a person possesses is relatively small; (2) all men everywhere possessed the same values to different degrees; (3) values are organized into value systems; (4) the antecedents of human values can be traced to culture, society and its institutions, and*

personality; (5) the consequences of human values will be manifested in virtually all phenomena that social scientists might consider worth investigating and understanding (Rokeach, 1973, p. 3).

Regardless of cultural differences, Rokeach assumed that all human beings share the same small set of values. The only difference, apparently, lies in the matter of the degree to which the values are subscribed, not the values *per se*. In addition to that, the assumption regarding antecedents of values includes personality, allowing for individual differences in values and value systems. Arrangement of values into systems is also universal. Individuals arrange culturally derived values in terms of relative importance to them; that is, they create hierarchies of values. It seems that, for Rokeach, the values themselves do not change across cultures and individuals, but rather their places vary in an individual's hierarchical systems. Lastly, values are of paramount importance in human functioning, suggesting that "social scientists" must pay greater attention to them.

Nature of Values: Definition of Terms

Rokeach (1973) proposed the following definitions of value and value system:

A value is an enduring belief that a specific mode of conduct or end-state of existence is personally or socially preferable to an opposite or converse mode of conduct or end-state of existence. A value system is an enduring organization of beliefs concerning preferable modes of conduct or end states of existence along a continuum of relative importance. (p. 5)

Rokeach elaborated upon his conceptualization of values under these headings: beliefs; endurance, relativity, and conflicts; hierarchy; types; and, standards.

Beliefs. Values are *prescriptive or proscriptive beliefs* indicating whether experiences and results of actions are desirable or undesirable. As beliefs, values are comprised of cognitive, affective, and behavioral components. A value is a cognition relating to desirability of experiences. It represents knowing both the correctness of current behavior as well as the end state, or life goals, for which to strive. A value is affective in that it generates emotions. Behavior inconsistent with values may lead to negative emotions. Strongly held values may elicit negative emotions towards people who do not uphold them. A value is an intervening variable influencing behavior.

Endurance, Relativity and Conflicts. Values are both enduring and relative. The enduring quality of values is explained by how values are initially taught to children. Rokeach proposes that values endure because they are initially taught through socialization practices in isolation from other values. When young people are taught values, they are presented as absolute and unchanging, and without reference to other values. For example, with respect to honesty, children are taught it as an absolute. As Rokeach notes, they are not taught to be a little bit honest or sporadically so; nor is honesty taught by relating it to other values, such as politeness (which, at times, overrides honesty). It is the isolated and thus absolute learning of values that guarantees their endurance and stability. Paradoxically, as Rokeach stated, "there is also a relative quality of values that must be made explicit…" (p.6). The paradox of endurance and relativity of values is explained by children's maturation and increasing social experience. It seems that for Rokeach, the learned values themselves may endure, but their relative importance may change over time. As children mature, they are likely to encounter situations which involve more than one value—values conflicts—requiring decision making. In adolescence, for example, conflict may arise between the values of obedience and independence. To resolve the conflict, adolescents must decide which value is more important to them: obedience or independence. Their decision resolves the conflict, and the result influences not only their behavior but also the organization of their values.

Hierarchy. Values conflicts lead to the emergence of individuals' systems or hierarchies of values. Without the experience of such conflicts, learned values would remain as they were taught to children: isolated and absolute. Movement through life stages ensures that this is not the case. In Rokeach's own words:

> *Gradually, through experience and a process of maturation, we all learn to integrate the isolated, absolute values we have been taught in this or that context into a hierarchically organized system, wherein each value is ordered in priority or importance relative to other values.* (p. 6).

Types. The theory of human values proposes two main categories of values: terminal and instrumental. As noted earlier, Rokeach assumed that there are a relatively small number of values. He identified 18 values for each category, see Table 9, which are incorporated into his Survey of Human Values.

Table 9. Rokeach's Terminal and Instrumental Values

Terminal	Instrumental
A comfortable life	Ambitious
An exciting life	Broadminded
A sense of accomplishment	Capable
A world at peace	Cheerful
A world of beauty	Clean
Equality	Courageous
Family security	Forgiving
Freedom	Helpful
Happiness	Honest
Inner harmony	Imaginative
Mature love	Independent
National security	Intellectual
Pleasure	Logical
Salvation	Loving
Self-respect	Obedient
Social recognition	Polite
True friendship	Responsible
Wisdom	Self-controlled
Note: Adapted from table of values, Rokeach, 1973, p. 28.	

Terminal values refer to desirable end states of existence; *instrumental values* refer to beliefs regarding desirable modes of conduct.

The theory proposes two kinds of values for each category (see Table 10). Terminal values are classified as *personal* and *social*. Inner harmony and a comfortable life are examples of personal terminal values. On the other hand, a world at peace and equality are examples of social terminal values.

Table 10. A Sample of Rokeach's Terminal and Instrumental Values Presented in Their Respective Sub-Categories

Terminal		Instrumental	
Personal	Social	Moral	Competence/ Self Actualization
Inner harmony (freedom from inner conflict)	A world at peace (freedom of war and conflict)	Forgiving (Willing to pardon others)	Capable (Competent, effective)
A Comfortable life (a prosperous life)	Equality (equal opportunity for all)	Helpful (Working for the welfare of others)	Independent (self-reliant, self-sufficient)
Self-respect (self-esteem)	National security (protection from attack)	Honest (sincere and truthful)	Intellectual (Intelligent, reflective)
Wisdom (a mature understanding of life)	World of beauty (a world of nature and the arts)	Responsible dependable, reliable)	Logical (Consistent, rational)
A sense of accomplishment (Lasting contribution)	True friendship (Close companionship)	Obedient (Dutiful, respectful)	Imaginative (Daring, creative)
Note: Selected Value terms with original descriptors in parentheses (Rokeach, 1973, p. 28			

Instrumental values are classified into *morality* and *competence*, the latter is also known as, *self-actualization*. Moral values are those that have an interpersonal focus. When these values are violated, feelings of guilt are the result. Moral values, with their social focus, are the prime concern of society because adherence to moral values benefits all individuals. "Forgiving" and "helpful" are examples of moral instrumental values. Competence/self-actualization values have a personal focus, concerned with self-efficacy, not morality. When competence values are violated, the result is feelings of shame about personal inadequacy. "Capable" and "independent" are examples of instrumental values of competence. (See Table 10 for additional examples of all four types of values). Rokeach illustrates the difference between values of morality and competence as follows: "[B]ehaving honestly and responsibly leads one to feel that he [or she] is behaving morally, whereas behaving logically, intelligently or imaginatively leads one to feel that he [or she] is behaving competently" (p.8).

Standards. Values are multifaceted standards that guide both behavioral and cognitive activities. Rokeach (1973) enumerates several ways that we use values as standards in our daily living. We employ values as standards in instances when we: take positions on social issues and favor a particular ideology; present ourselves to others; evaluate and judge self and others; compare ourselves with others to determine whether we are as moral and competent as others; rationalize our beliefs, attitudes and behaviors that are socially unacceptable. In effect, conceptualizing values as standards, directing a range of human phenomena, suggests the motivational quality of values.

Motivational Functions of Values

In addition to their cognitive, affective, and behavioral components, values are said to have a strong motivational component. Whether they are of the instrumental or terminal type, values motivate behavior associated with goal attainment and satisfying our needs. For example, the instrumental value of politeness motivates us to act courteously with others; the terminal value of accomplishment motivates us to approach tasks diligently. Values also influence how we meet our needs in daily life. Obedience, for example, will lead us to meet our needs in socially acceptable ways. While acknowledging the motivational function of instrumental and terminal values, Rokeach's primary concern is how values are used to address what he considers a fundamental psychological need—self-esteem. It is clear that in the theory of human values, values are subservient to self-esteem:

> *"They [Values] are in the final analysis the conceptual tools and weapons that we all employ in order to maintain and enhance self-esteem. They are in the service of what McDougall (1926) has called the master sentiment—the sentiment of self-regard"* (Rokeach, 1973p. 14).

To further emphasize the motivational role of values with respect to the self-regard need, Rokeach adds: "[A]ll of a person's values are conceived to maintain and enhance the master sentiment of self-regard by helping a person adjust to his society, defend his ego against threat, and test reality" (p. 15). Rokeach elaborates on how values maintain and enhance self-regard/self-esteem by discussing three motivational functions of values: adjustive, ego-defensive, and self-actualization.

Adjustive function. Self-esteem is maintained and enhanced by adhering to values that are oriented to adjusting to societal prescriptions. Instrumental values (such as getting along well with others, politeness, and self-control), and terminal values (such as success and prestige) are likely to motivate actions consistent with societal expectations. Clearly, the values manifesting this adjustment and orientation may be conceived as a subset of the overarching value, namely, compliance with societal prescriptions. By conforming to societal standards, negative feedback, in the form of criticism, is avoided, thereby maintaining, if not enhancing, one's self-esteem.

Ego-defensive function. Through this motivational function, individuals use values to maintain self-esteem when acknowledging that the reality of a situation is personally threatening. Rokeach draws upon psychoanalytic theory to explain how values serve an ego-defensive function. Rationalization, a Freudian ego-defense mechanism, transforms unacceptable needs, emotions, and actions into acceptable forms. He notes that "values are ready-made concepts provided by our culture to ensure that such justifications proceed smoothly and effortlessly. All instrumental and terminal values may be employed to serve ego-defensive functions…" (p. 15).

Rokeach provides examples of the use of values in rationalization: unkind remarks to a friend may be rationalized as honest communication; inhibited sex life is rationalized as a life guided by self-control; an act of aggression by a nation is rationalized as national security. Values are indispensable for the process of the ego-defensive mechanism of rationalization: "The process of rationalization, so crucial a component in virtually all defense mechanism, would be impossible if man did not possess values to rationalize with" (p. 13). As such, values serve to maintain and enhance self-esteem.

Self-actualization function. As the term implies, this form of the motivational function of values leads to enhancement of self-esteem. This function is also known as the *knowledge* function, which includes the search for meaning and the need to understand and improve one's mental organization of perceptions and beliefs. Both knowledge and (Maslow's) self-actualization are implicated in some instrumental and terminal values. Individuals are said to value such end-states as wisdom, feeling of accomplishment, independence, and consistency. It is assumed that everyone possesses such values, though people differ with respect to the importance they place on them. In fact, relative importance extends of all functions of values: some people may place more importance on adjustment-oriented values, while others focus on knowledge-oriented values.

Of the three motivational functions of values concerned with self-esteem, only the knowledge function, or self-actualization, relates to enhancement of it by fostering authentic personal growth. The adjustive function and ego defensive functions represent maintenance of self-esteem. Adjustive function maintains current level of self-esteem by mindless conformity to societal values; ego-defensive function does so by engaging in justification of breaches of values. Enhancement of self-esteem by adjustive or ego-defensive function results in a false level of positive self-esteem.

The theory of human values proposes that the three forms of motivational functions of values operate in all individuals. As with values themselves, the relative importance individuals attribute to the three functions may change from time to time. Relative importance is the essential characteristic of value systems.

Hierarchies of Values: Mechanisms of Change

It is unusual, if not rare, that the variety of people's behaviors is guided by a single value; it is more likely that clusters of values influence people's actions. According to Rokeach, these clusters are organized into hierarchies whose ordering may change over time. A value system contains enduring values, though their position on the hierarchy changes. Therefore, value systems are described as both stable and unstable:

> *Once a value is learned it becomes integrated into an organized system of values wherein each value is ordered in priority with respect to other values. Such relative conception of values enables us to define change as a reordering of priorities and, at the same time, to see the total value system as relatively stable over time. It is stable enough to reflect the fact of sameness and continuity of a unique personality socialized within a given culture and society, yet unstable enough to permit rearrangements of value priorities as a result of changes in culture, society, and personal experience.* (p. 11)

Organization of values into a ranked order system is not simply an academic exercise. Value systems (hierarchies) serve the important function of conflict resolution. It is common for individuals to encounter situations that activate two or more incompatible values in a system. Situations may create conflict, for example, between obedience and independence, hedonic pleasure and religious strictures, and self-respect and the approval of others. The existence of a hierarchy of values enables individuals to decide between alternatives and to resolve conflicts. Reordering the relative importance of values when confronted with a values conflict is a conflict-resolution process.

Value systems also assist in other forms of conflict, those involving contradiction between value and behavior. Contradictions occur when individuals behave contrary to their values: lying instead of being honest, being selfish instead of charitable, being rude instead of polite.

Some of these conflicts have little impact on individuals' psychological states; other conflicts may create intense psychological distress. The conflict resulting from contradiction may be resolved by a lowering of the importance of the value involved or by altering behavior to be consisted with the espoused value. Resolving contradictions becomes more difficult when the value involved is central to an individual's self-conception. If the value of honesty is high in hierarchical order, and deemed an important part of self-concept, resolution using rationalization becomes more challenging. The theory of human values explains the difficulty by referring to the proposition of values as standards.

As standards used in self-evaluation, values are inextricably bound to self-concept. When our self-concept, including our perception of our attitudes and behaviors, is consistent with our values, we feel a sense of self-satisfaction. However, conflict between behavior and values, or between two or more values, negatively affect self-concept. For example, situations that activate a value conflict between self-respect and independence, are manifested in reevaluating self-perception: "What kind of person am I?" Similarly, self-perception is implicated when behavior contradicts a value of achievement, such as when pleasure-seeking overtakes achievement-oriented behavior. When such contradictions involve self-concept, the result is varying levels of psychological distress. In the theory of human values, the distress produced by contradictions implicating self-concept is termed *self-dissatisfaction*.

Self-dissatisfaction

Rokeach described self-dissatisfaction as:

> ...*a dissatisfaction arising from some cognitive discrepancy between self-conceptions and performance in each situation or class of situations. Does my total performance in this situation—what I said, what I did, and most important, what it signifies about myself—measure up to whatever conception I have of myself as a competent person? As a moral person? Most, if not all, activities a person engages in end, at least implicitly, with some evaluation of his performance. To the extent that a person perceives a discrepancy between self-conceptions and performance, he experiences it emotionally as...a state of self-dissatisfaction.* (p. 226).

Self-dissatisfaction is situational, arising from the awareness of contradictions. Such awareness leads to a process of self-evaluation, in which values, as standards, serve as criteria for self-judgement. Self-dissatisfaction may create enormous distress in the form of anxiety, depression, internal conflict, disaffection, and alienation from society.

Sources of self-dissatisfaction. Feelings of self-dissatisfaction arise when values relating to competence or morality are contradicted by one's behavior, triggering negative self-evaluation. Self-judgments of incompetency in a situation result from assessments of deficiencies in, for example, skill, intelligence, or "inability to play assigned roles in society successfully" (p. 228). Self-judgements of immorality result from, for example, perceptions of harming others or self, and lack of impulse control regarding thoughts, emotions or behavior. Rokeach notes that society dictates standards of competence and morality, which are used by individuals for the purpose of self-evaluation:

> *In the final analysis, society and its agencies have the most say in defining general standards of competence and morality and the conceptions that a person has about his own competence and morality. Society defines the many ways of becoming competent and moral, rewards their positive manifestations, and punishes their negative manifestations. Society moreover defines the roles that people play, sets standards of competence and morality in playing these roles, and rewards and punishes conformity and nonconformity to such standards. A person learns to evaluate his own performance and those of others for competence and morality by social comparison processes....* (p. 228)

Contravention of the dictates of society, is, ultimately, the general source of self-dissatisfaction.

Reduction of Self-dissatisfaction. In general, there are two methods by which reduction of self-dissatisfaction can be achieved: denial or growth. Denial may take the form of repression or suppression. Repression, an unconscious process, prevents the contradiction to rise to the level of awareness, or simply blocks the contradiction at the point of initial occurrence. Suppression, on the other hand is a conscious process leading to active denial of the importance of the contradiction.

Rokeach does not view self-dissatisfaction as entirely negative in nature. States of self-dissatisfaction may be stimuli for personal growth. Rather than denial of the contradiction, it is brought to full awareness. Psychological distress has the potential to motivate individuals to restore consistency between the psychological components creating the state of dissonance. In situations creating a behavior-values discrepancy, behavior may be changed to reflect values, or vice versa. The relative importance of values, that is, their place in one's hierarchy, may be adjusted upward or downward to match one's behavior. Similarly, with situations involving aspects of self-concept and behavior and/or values, either component can be adjusted to regain a balance between components. Generally, though, personal growth is the product of adjusting one's behavior to match the value in question. Personal growth that self-dissatisfaction motivates, in fact, ensures that one's activities comply with societal values.

Summary. The theory of human values proposes a small number of universal values that are organized into two categories: instrumental and terminal. All values are the product of socialization of individuals through child-rearing practices and their involvement with societal institutions such as schools. With maturation and increased interaction with the social environment, situations arise which lead to values conflicts. The distress produced threatens an individual's self-esteem, which Rokeach views as a fundamental psychological need. In Rokeach's theory, the primary role of values in daily living is the maintenance and enhancement of self-esteem. Three functions of values serve to maintain and enhance self-esteem: ego-defense, adjustment, and self-actualization. Values, then, are subservient to self-esteem.

An important cognitive process proposed to address values conflicts is arranging learned values hierarchically. According to the theory of human values individuals create hierarchies of values, using those that their society has adopted from Rokeach's small number of universal values. As the term implies, individuals arrange their learned values in terms of their perceived importance at particular points in time. As a result, there is a plurality of hierarchies—the ranking of the importance of values taught in a society varies among individuals in that society; position of values in a hierarchy also changes from time to time for each individual. A hierarchy of values is a flexible cognitive structure used to make decisions during the occurrence of conflict arising from situations that activate two values, or contradictions between value and behavior. Conflict involving two competing values, or inconsistency between value and behavior, produces negative emotions, including anxiety and depression. The higher the relative importance of a value in one's hierarchy, the greater is its importance to one's self-concept. When a conflict involves a contradiction between a higher order value and behavior, intense distress results, creating a condition called self-dissatisfaction. Feelings of self-dissatisfaction arise when behavior contradicts values relating to competence or morality, triggering negative self-evaluation. The standards used in self-evaluation are those dictated by society, not those created by individuals themselves. The distress inherent in self-dissatisfaction can be an opportunity for personal growth by adjusting behavior to conform with societal expectations. Alternatively, denial of the conflict, in the form of repression or suppression, prevents or eliminates the distress associated with self-dissatisfaction, thus maintaining the *status quo*. Hierarchies of values, like values themselves, are instruments subservient to the primary psychological need: the maintenance and enhancement of self-esteem.

Dąbrowski's Hierarchy of Values

To say that *hierarchy of values* is a critical component in the theory of positive disintegration is to underestimate its importance to the theory. In fact, development of a hierarchy of values, and advanced development are synonymous (Tillier, 2018). The hierarchy of values, created through the process of positive disintegration, ranks values from lower moral functioning to higher moral functioning. As such, there are values associated with each of the five levels of development. A Dąbrowskian hierarchy is created by the resolution of general inner conflict produced by the discrepancy between the way the world ought to be and the way it is. Specifically, the experience of disintegrating dynamisms of spontaneous multilevel disintegration (Level III) can be described as an increase in one's awareness of one's personal values that are in conflict with ideal values; that is, the inner conflict of Level III is a values conflict. The orderly arrangement of a set of values into what is lower versus what is higher leads to the creation of a hierarchy of values, which begins the resolution of inner conflict. In a sense, signs of advanced development are the creation of higher moral values and the manifestation of those values in behavior.

Development and Values

The nature of valuation changes with the progression from primary integration to secondary integration. Specifically, what is appraised as valuable in advanced development is qualitatively different than what is considered worthwhile in primary integration. As mental development progresses from primitive to advanced, the nature of valuation changes accordingly. Both development and a hierarchy of values are the products of positive disintegration, as noted by Tillier (2018):

> *One of the most important milestones of development is the emergence of the hierarchization of values. Initially, our value structures are heavily determined by our socialization and there is little differentiation of values. The experiences of positive disintegration create grave doubts: existential feelings of angst and hopelessness and perhaps even suicidal feelings over the meaning and sense of life. These experiences challenge and eventually overwhelm the ability of our socialized values to explain and cope with life, often creating a feeling of disconnection.* Tillier (2018, p. 176)

Unlike socialized values which are learned, in the theory of positive disintegration values are created by the transformation of the primitive quality of functions. Creation of values is the product of the activity of dynamisms, the forces of positive disintegration. Dynamisms transform each function from its primitive manifestation in primary integration to its advanced state in secondary integration, and then, into increasingly developed, inclusive moral values.

Dąbrowski et al. (1970) explain how positive disintegration creates a hierarchy of values by using four functions—self-preservation, syntony and empathy, sexual instinct, and attitude towards death—to illustrate the process.

Self-preservation instinct. At the level of primary integration, self-preservation is manifested in uncontrollable fear or aggression when there is perception of threat to self; it is not modulated by self-awareness or awareness of others. In Level II, unilevel disintegration, the force of the instinct is less impulsive, with periods of hesitation and weakened aggression, and affected by the dynamisms of ambivalence and ambitendency. In spontaneous multilevel disintegration, Level III, the primitive manifestations of self-preservation begin to wane. The focus of preservation or defense, which was originally exclusively oneself, now extends to include family, friends, and people in general. At this level, self-preservation is organized into a hierarchy of values. In Level IV, organized multilevel disintegration, the primitive manifestations are eliminated. The focus of self-preservation is now on preservation of one's higher personality traits. Development of these traits becomes associated with the dynamism of self-perfection. There is a broadening of the desire to protect that includes deep patriotism and cultural accomplishments. In secondary integration, Level V, self-preservation is transformed into a function of personality. Self-preservation now serves to protect those traits that appear as immutable values. The culmination of the transformation of self-preservation is its merging with self-perfection, with feelings of connection to all people and all creatures. In this way, the self-preservation instinct that is initially and exclusively self-focused with associated strong, aggressive responses to threat (real or imaginary), is qualitatively altered. It serves to protect not oneself from harm, but rather to protect humanity, other living beings, and cultural accomplishments.

Syntony and empathy. Original manifestations of syntony (temperamental response to environment) consist of nonreflective emotional contagion, and gregariousness of a reflective form, manifesting an ability to understand others, culminating in a deeply empathic approach to people. With empathy comes the understanding of the needs of others leading to a desire to help, guided by kindness and generosity.

Sexual instinct. As a biological force, in its primitive form this instinct represents a strong drive that may reach such intensity that it proves difficult to control. As a result, there is a disregard of faithfulness or quality of personal relationships. Faithfulness to a partner or inhibition of the sexual impulse occurs primarily due to societal pressures or fear of punishment. At the primitive level, concerns relating to satisfaction of the sexual instinct relate to avoidance of social disapproval, punishment, and embarrassment. With subsequent higher levels of development, more cognitive processing is involved, beginning with ambivalence, for example, between satisfaction and inhibition, faithfulness and infidelity. There is awareness of a growing need for exclusiveness and fidelity in sexual relationships. Gradually, sexual experience becomes a creative element, not simply a biological drive that needs gratification.

Attitude toward death. At a primitive level, there is no indication of understanding of death. Awareness of the possibility of death produces strong defensive responses to the terror and panic that accompany such experiences. As with the functions of the self-preservation and sexual instincts, the foundation for transformation is the experience of ambivalence, in Level II, which ranges from anxiety and rationalization to indifference. Death is perceived as external to life and, therefore, the idea of death is not integrated within the concept of self. With multilevel disintegration, Level III, there is a gradual integration into the overall personality structure. Death is thought of as one of many human problems, albeit the most important one. The problem of death gains a high level of relative importance manifested by the value attributed to things, which is determined from the perspective of death. In fact, the meaning of life itself is considered from the point of view of death. It's place in the hierarchy of values is shared with other higher values, such as responsibility for others and charity. At the highest levels of development, Level IV/V, the problem of death is subordinated to other problems; it becomes part of the process of inner development.

Table 11 summarizes Dąbrowski's use of the four functions—self-preservation, syntony and empathy, sexual instinct, and attitude towards death—to demonstrate the process of creating a hierarchy of values. The process of positive disintegration, through the work of dynamisms, transforms the initial primitive operations of the four functions associated with primary integration into positive values, associated with secondary integration. Dąbrowski's the descriptors of the process are arranged from lowest to the highest, as indicated by the arrows for each function in the table. As related in the discussion of each function and illustrated in Table 11, creation of hierarchies represent progression through the Levels. While the table includes only the lowest and highest levels, Levels II, III, and IV are implied.

Table 11. Hierarchies of Values for Self-Preservation, Syntony and Empathy, Sexual Instinct, and attitude toward death

Function	Hierarchies of values	Level of Development
Self-preservation	• Protection of humanity and all living things	Secondary Integration V
	• Protect one's traits that are values	
	• Deep patriotism	
	• Family friends and people in general	
	• Perception of threat and uncontrollable fear or aggression	Primary Integration I
Syntony and empathy	• Kindness and generosity	Secondary Integration V
	• Desire to help others	
	• Understanding others	
	• Gregariousness	
	• Emotional contagion	Primary Integration I
Sexual instinct	• Exclusiveness and fidelity in relationships	Secondary Integration V
	• Inhibition	
	• Satisfaction	Primary Integration I
Attitude towards death	• Part of the process of development	Secondary Integration V
	• Meaning of life from the point of view of death	
	• Value of things perceived tom the perspective of death	
	• Seen as one of many human problems	
	• Disconnected from life	
	• Source of anxiety	
	• Strong defensive responses to the idea	Primary Integration I

As seen in Table 11, there is a separate hierarchy for each function. An implication of Dąbrowski's explanation is that, in the course of achieving one's final hierarchy of values, the transformational process (illustrated in Table 11) is repeated with other primitive behavioral and cognitive functions. In the theory of positive disintegration, reference is made to the creation of a single hierarchy of values that is synonymous with advanced development. My conjecture is that, as development progresses to the advanced Levels discrete hierarchies that are created by positive disintegration, are coalesced into one overarching hierarchy of values.

The preceding explanation of the creation of the hierarchies relating to the four functions is descriptive in nature, to illustrate the process of hierarchization of values. However, it must be remembered that the experience of the process is not one of abstract creation, but rather one that is fraught with intense, negative experiences of inner conflict, characteristic of Level III. In Level IV (organized multilevel disintegration), the lower forms in the hierarchy are eliminated, and the positive moral values remain. The discussion of the four functions thus illustrates how *hierarchy of values* and *development* are synonymous:

> *To each level of mental development there is a corresponding level of value experience. Mental development of man and the development of a hierarchy of values are, in fact, two names for the same process. One cannot separate the two. [W]e can distinguish five levels of development of emotional and instinctive functions and five corresponding levels of experience of values.* (Dąbrowski, 1970, p. 98)

At the highest level of development, the theory of positive disintegration stipulates that there are values that are shared by individuals who are at the pinnacle of development.

> *It is characteristic that…moral judgments made by individuals representing a very high level of universal mental development display a very high degree of agreement. Let us recall Socrates who died as a result of injustice and Gandhi who died as a result of violence. Both forgave those who killed them.* (p. 92).

Hierarchy of Values and Hierarchy of Aims

In the theory of positive disintegration, the values created by the transformation of functions (e.g., self-preservation, syntony, sexual instincts, and attitude towards death) are referred to as hierarchy of *actual* values. Actual hierarchy of values is contrasted with a *prospective* hierarchy of values, termed *hierarchy of aims*, which is a continuation and development of the presently possessed hierarchy of values. Whereas hierarchy of values refers to values currently constructed, hierarchy of aims represents aspirational values, ideals to which individuals strive. In a sense, the hierarchy of aims represents a program for self-perfection. Once individuals understand what higher levels of a function are (e.g., self-preservation develops into preservation of all living beings), they become objectives—aims—of further development. Hierarchy of aims is a continuation and development of a hierarchy of values.

It is important to note that for Dąbrowski "higher levels of mental development become values that people strive to attain." (p. 105). As such, it is Level III (spontaneous multilevel disintegration) that signals the beginning of the construction of a hierarchy of values. A hierarchy of values, the basis for a hierarchy of aims, emerges with the dynamisms of Level IV (organized multilevel disintegration), especially with the dynamism of authentism:

> *[A] hierarchy of values appears at an advanced stage. The beginnings of mental development have a spontaneous character and only at a later stage, with the initiation of reflection, self-control, inner psychic transformation, and authentism, does a hierarchy of values begin to emerge. It is with the dynamism of authentism that arises a sense of responsibility and the need to apply in every human problem a hierarchy of values and a hierarchy of aims. In consequence, the need to bring about in oneself and in others the realization of this hierarchy of aims is the outcome of the dynamism of authentism.* (Dąbrowski, 1970, p. 106-107)

Authentism (also termed authenticity), a dynamism of the highest level of development (Level IV/V), is a critical developmental force. In the theory of positive disintegration authentism is defined as:

> ...*a dynamism which consists in the feeling awareness and expression of one's own emotional, intellectual, and volitional attitudes, achieved through autonomous developmental transformations of one's own hierarchy of values and aims. It involves a high degree of insight into oneself. Authenticity is a symptom of independence from lower instinctive levels and selective independence from influences of the external environment and the inner psychic milieu. It brings about a high degree of unity of one's thinking, emotions, and activity. Authentism involves conscious activity in accordance with one's inner truth. The appearance and growth of authentism results from the operation of such dynamisms as dissatisfaction with oneself, autonomy, the third factor, positive maladjustment, ' subject object' in oneself, inner psychic transformation and the personality ideal* (Dąbrowski et al., 1970, p.163).

Summary. Hierarchy of values and advanced development are synonymous. Values in the theory of positive disintegration are not those taught through socialization, but rather they are created by positive disintegration. Dynamisms operate to transform original primitive manifestations of functions into increasingly higher moral values in the levels of development beginning with Level III (spontaneous multilevel disintegration). In the theory of positive disintegration, constructing a hierarchy of values is illustrated using four functions: self-preservation, syntony and empathy, sexual instinct, and attitude towards death. Creation of a hierarchy of values for each function represents a transformation of their experience throughout the five levels of development, ranging from primary to secondary integration. Self-preservation is transformed from aggression and fear to preservation of personality traits, and to connection with people in general. Syntony is transformed from superficial emotional ties to people and gregariousness to genuine empathy with the motivation to help others with kindness. Sexual instinct is transformed from drive gratification to a creative element. Attitude towards death is transformed from elicitation of angst to understanding death in the context of the meaning of life. Different values are associated with different levels of development, such that a higher level of development has corresponding higher complexity and moral value. The highest moral values are combined with the dynamisms of Level IV (organized multilevel disintegration), such as self-perfection.

An established hierarchy of values is only evident at the highest level of development, with the emergence of the dynamism of authentism. Authentism, a Level IV dynamism, emerges from such organized multilevel disintegration dynamisms as dissatisfaction with oneself, autonomy, the third factor, and inner psychic transformation. A hierarchy of values refers to actual values, which are currently part of individuals; a hierarchy of aims refers to prospective values, that is, values which are aspirational. As such, they represent a program of further growth for individuals. Hierarchies of values and aims manifest the highest level of development in the theory of positive disintegration. At that level, values drive daily behavior.

Rokeach and Dąbrowski

A comparison of Rokeach's theory of human values and Dąbrowski's treatment of values reveals some superficial similarities and profound differences. Both approaches agree that: values are beliefs that certain modes of conduct are more desirable than others; values are standards against which behavior and self are evaluated; value conflicts occur resulting in psychological distress; values are motivational, and values are organized into hierarchies.

Readers familiar with the theory of positive disintegration likely have already identified the most significant factor that differentiates Dąbrowski's from Rokeach's perspective. Framed in Dąbrowskian terms, Rokeach's explanation of both the formation of values and the resolution of values conflicts emphasizes the pivotal role of the social environment. In the theory of positive disintegration, the social environment but one of the three factors of development, the other two are the first factor, biology: and the third factor, autonomous forces. The second factor serves to contain the extreme impulsivity of biological instincts and drives, whose expressions are moderated by the demands of societal prescriptions. Compliance with societal norms and expectations is characteristic of second factor development. Central components of Rokeach's theory describe the essence of second factor development: values are not conceived of as individuals' values but rather as those taught by society's agents of socialization, with which individuals are expected to comply. Society doles out rewards for compliance, punishment for non-compliance.

Both Rokeach and Dąbrowski acknowledge the inevitability of conflict between values and between values and behavior. How the conflicts are resolved is dramatically different in the two approaches. In the theory of human values, conflict between two values is resolved by change in the relative importance of values in the hierarchy—which value becomes higher in importance depends on the situation. In the theory of positive disintegration, resolution is accomplished by accepting the higher moral value and rejecting the lower, regardless of the situation. Conflict between values and behaviors tends to produce varying levels of distress. Rokeach, like Dąbrowski, notes that individuals resolve conflicts by changing their behaviors to be consistent with the values involved. Like Dąbrowski, Rokeach agrees that such conflicts are opportunities for personal growth. However, Rokeach also includes the possibility of an individual's use of rationalization to alleviate discomfort produced—the ego-defensive motivation of values—that is alien to the theory of positive disintegration.

That conflict between values and behaviors can create intense psychological distress is another point of agreement. Such distress occurs when the discrepancy involves values that are central to one's self-concept. It is ironic to encounter the term that Rokeach uses to describe such distress—*self-dissatisfaction*. There are similarities to *dissatisfaction with self* in terms of the negative experience, but not in how the distress is lessened or resolved. Consistent with other aspects of the theory of human values, the prescription for dealing with self-dissatisfaction is anchored to the social environment: it requires compliance.

Though both approaches use a hierarchy *of values*, their individual conceptions demonstrate additional dramatic differences. In the theory of human values, hierarchization is a rather straightforward matter of organizing values, learned initially from caregivers, into a system of relative importance. Rokeach's hierarchy of values is a *simple utilitarian construction* which emerges from situations in which two values are in conflict. The hierarchy of values is a device for resolving values conflicts: it enables changes in relative importance. Furthermore, for Rokeach the device is a common feature of most if not all human beings. In stark contrast, Dąbrowski's hierarchy of values is forged by the inner conflict experienced by individuals, leading them to transform their primitive manifestation of functions to higher moral values. It is not a device to resolve values conflicts by simply changing the relative importance of values: Dąbrowski's hierarchy of values is a product of the *transformation of lower primitive instincts*, drives and needs into complex, other-oriented, morally higher values. As such, a hierarchy of values is a construction that appears only at the higher levels of development and therefore it is not common to all human beings.

From a Dąbrowskian point of view, Rokeach's approach to human values is comparable to Level I (primary integration), but it is not the values themselves that leads me to that association. It is the proposed origin of individuals' values and the expectation to comply with them. For Rokeach, honesty and kindness, for example, are the product of socialization along with the requirement to comply with all socially prescribed values that differentiates Rokeach from Dąbrowski, not the values themselves. If individuals simply adopt societal values without question and are motivated to comply with them for fear of negative consequences, then, they are likely at the level of primary integration. However, it must be emphasized that this interpretation does not mean that they are bad people! I surmise that Dąbrowski might say that Rokeach's conceptualization of values is consistent with Dąbrowski's view of normal development:

> *By this [normal development] we mean a type of development which is most common, and which entails the least amount of inner conflict and of psychological*

transformation. Development is limited to the maturational stages of human life and to the innate psychological type of the individual (Dąbrowski, 1991, p. 20).

From a Dąbrowskian perspective, Rokeach's theory is useful because it is a detailed explanation of values in normal development. Its emphasis on compliance with socially derived values and lack of inner conflict (i.e., between the way the world ought to be and the way it is) aligns well with Level I (primary integration). The theory of human values, thus, describes in detail the automatic compliance to societal values that is transcended in the process of Dąbrowskian development.

Conclusions

Rokeach's proposal of how a hierarchy of values is constructed is, in part, analogous to its construction in the theory of positive disintegration. The similarity lies in the Rokeach's concept of self-dissatisfaction. Intense psychological distress is produced by an individual's awareness of a discrepancy between what they hold dear with respect to self-definition and awareness of how their behavior contradicts values that are central to their self-concept. Psychological distress manifested by depression and anxiety motivates individuals to resolve the contradiction. Though Rokeach does not use the phrase *inner conflict*, that is, in fact, what is part of the experience of self-dissatisfaction. So far, this process is similar, if not identical, to dissatisfaction with oneself. The similarity also includes the resolution of the discrepancy that is causing distress—adjusting behavior so that it is consistent with the value(s) involved.

It is difficult to see the difference between Rokeach and Dąbrowski with respect to the dissatisfaction concept unless we view their positions from the point of view of motivation. The motivation for resolution of self-dissatisfaction –to feel better about oneself—stems from a condition of low self-esteem. Rokeach places a great deal of importance on the need for positive self-regard or esteem. In order to regain self-regard, individuals' change their behavior to match the value to avoid punishment by the social environment. On the other hand, Dąbrowski's dissatisfaction with *self* signals the beginning of establishing a hierarchy of values, *motivated not by enhancement of self-esteem or by avoiding punishment, but rather by the desire to become a better person.*

It seems to me that a Rokeachian conceptualization of values is the starting point for Dąbrowski's hierarchy of values. Socialization is a universal process by which individuals *learn the norms and values of the society* in which they live. *Compliance* is an important value that is taught initially by parents and care givers and later by teachers and other members of societal institutions. The initial stages of a set of values forged by positive disintegration lies in the erosion of the conditioned response of unthinking compliance with societal demands. This is necessary to set the foundation for the actual construction of a hierarchy of values—the transformation of primitive functions to higher moral values.

In the theory of positive disintegration, the established hierarchy of values is, in fact, a combination of the values constructed through the transformation of functions such as self-preservation instinct, described earlier. As individuals become aware of the distinction between the higher forms and lower forms of a function, lower forms are rejected while higher forms—values—are embraced and manifested in daily living. With the establishment of a hierarchy of values comes the desire for enhanced self-improvement thereby creating an additional hierarchy, one of aims. Developed hierarchies of values and aims are part of Level IV, organized multilevel disintegration. It seems that the hierarchies are separate from the dynamisms of Level IV. I find this quite interesting since the labels of the dynamisms seem to me to represent values e.g., responsibility for self and others and empathy) and aims (e.g., education of self and autopsychotherapy).

Thus, a question arises: does hierarchy vanish with the achievement of Level IV? If developmental dynamisms are manifested in daily living, it seems that the lower levels of functions have been eliminated from individuals' thinking and behaving. It leads me to wonder whether the hierarchies are a means to an end with Levels IV and V being the ends.

CHAPTER 11
Mental Health

It is not surprising that Dąbrowski was very concerned with mental health. After all, he was a practicing psychiatrist who held top administrative positions in mental health institutions. His keen interest is manifested from the outset in his theorizing. After the first known publication of his theory in 1946, "Psychic Integration and Disintegration", he published "The Concept of Mental Health" in 1948 (Kawczak, 1970). Regrettably, both publications are available only in Polish. Fortunately, his first English language book, *Positive Disintegration* (Dąbrowski, 1964) contains an in-depth treatment of his position on mental health, which continues in subsequent English language books, culminating in one of his last books, published posthumously in Poland in 1996 "Poszukiwaniu *Zdrowia Psychicznego* [*In Search of Mental Health*]" (Mika, 2008, p. 139). Reflective of his perspective on mental health and its prominent position in the theory of positive disintegration, Dąbrowski's theory could easily be renamed a theory of *positive mental health*.

Dąbrowski does not typically use the descriptor *positive* in his discussions of mental health, though he apparently was aware of its use. The phrase *positive mental health* is usually associated with the work of Marie Jahoda, whose 1958 book, "Current Concepts of Positive Mental Health" is a classic text that influenced subsequent definitions of mental health. Dąbrowski was not only aware of Jahoda's work but was also influenced by it (Tillier, 2018). Though *positive mental health* itself does not appear in Dąbrowski's books, his approach, with its emphasis on development, is certainly reflective of the intent of the phrase. A perusal of Jahoda (1958), when contrasted with Dąbrowski's conception of mental health, suggests some areas of agreement, but also significant disagreement. As expected, contrasting the two approaches reveals the uniqueness of Dąbrowskian mental health.

Jahoda's Critique of Concepts Used to Define Mental Health

Jahoda (1958) is a final report of an investigation of mental health ordered by the US commission on health, chaired by Marie Jahoda. On its face, it is typical, summarizing meetings with committee members and eminent individuals in the field, offering results of a comprehensive review of literature, and giving recommendations for research and practice. More importantly, the content of the report was groundbreaking: its articulate critique of the established approach y to mental health, and her proposal of novel criteria to define mental health, represents a radical departure from thinking at the time. In the 1950s, mental health was considered to be the absence of mental illness: "Mental health as the opposite of mental disease is perhaps the most widespread and apparently simplest attempt at definition" (Jahoda, 1958, p. 10). She criticizes this simple definition along with two other popular criteria for defining mental health: wellbeing and normality.

Criticism of a definition of mental health as the *absence of mental illness* rests on the fact that mental illness itself is difficult to define. It did not make sense to Jahoda to use an ill-defined concept to define another concept. What makes mental illness difficult to define is that determining what constitute illness is based on appraisal of behaviors. Jahoda pointed out that appraisal of actions "*as sick, normal or extraordinary in a positive sense often depends largely on accepted social conditions*" (italics in original, p. 13). Her message was that "accepted social conditions"—cultural and societal norms and values—must be considered when determining whether behaviors indicate mental illness. Values and norms vary not only at the macro level of society, but also within various societal groups, including families.

While the idea that mental illness is culturally bound was novel in the 1950s, it is interesting to note that it is accepted in present day by the psychiatric establishment. The American Psychiatric Association

(APA) currently instructs practitioners to consider *accepted social conditions* in the process of diagnosis. The current DSM 5 (Diagnostic and Statistical Manual 5, APA, 2013) states:

> *Mental disorders are defined in relation to cultural, social, and familial norms and values. Culture provides interpretive frameworks that shape the experience and expression of the symptoms, signs, and behaviors that are criteria for diagnosis. Culture is transmitted, revised, and recreated within the family and other social systems and institutions. Diagnostic assessment must therefore consider whether an individual's experiences, symptoms, and behaviors differ from sociocultural norms and lead to difficulties in adaptation in the cultures of origin and in specific social or familial contexts.* (p. 14)

Jahoda also rejected *states of well-being* as a suitable criterion to define mental health. This is surprising, given the current popularity of *wellness* in conceptions of mental health. Jahoda objected to mental health definitions that include terms such as *happiness, emotional wellbeing,* and *satisfaction with life*. Like dismissing the use of illness to define health, Jahoda argued that using the terminology of wellbeing, for which there is no consensus, to arrive at a definition of mental health is illogical. Jahoda further argued that states of well-being, such as happiness and unhappiness, are not only under the control of individuals, they are also influenced by external events. She reasoned those states of well-being can only be used as indicators of mental health if they are conceived of as personality attributes, rather than transient feelings: "To regard the *unhappy disposition* as a criterion of poor mental health is one thing. To regard *unhappiness*, regardless of the circumstances in which it occurs, as such an indicator is a different matter." (Jahoda, 1958, p. 20). Only when states of well-being are personality *predispositions* are they potentially useful criteria for defining mental health.

Normality is also viewed as an unsuitable criterion for mental health. There are two different concepts normality: statistical and prescriptive. Statistical normality distinguishes normal from abnormal behavior—mental health or mental illness—according to frequency in a population: frequent behaviors are normal; infrequent behaviors are abnormal. Statistical frequency is demonstrated by deviations from the mean in a bell curve: one standard deviation from the mean captures 68% of occurrences, while two standard deviations capture 95% of a population. Interestingly, the frequency or prevalence of virtually all mental disorders (according to the DSM-5) is approximately 5% or less: ADHD, 5% in children, 2.5% adults (p. 61); schizophrenia is 0.3%-0.7% (p. 102). To establish what is statistically normal, a population mean is essential. Arriving at a mean for biological or physical characteristics of a population, such as weight and height, is relatively straightforward, because they refer to universal properties of the entire human population and can be assessed using standard metrics. But when it comes to mental health and mental illness, no single population can be identified, because we are dealing with a human-generated socially constructed idea which varies among cultures. Jahoda therefore concludes that using statistical frequency to construct a conception of mental health is unsuitable.

Related to but different from the statistical frequency definition of normality is a prescriptive or normative one. While the statistical aspect describes the *actual* behavior of most of the population, the normative aspect prescribes how individuals *should* behave. Though these two aspects of normality may coincide, Jahoda cautioned against assuming they always do: "To believe that the two connotations [of normality] always coincide leads to the assertion that whatever exists in the majority of cases is right by virtue of its existence" (p. 15). What is correct behavior—the prescriptive aspect of normality—is determined by cultural norms. Accepting that correctness is culturally bound leads to questioning the value of the normative as a criterion of mental health.

Recently, Jaramillo and Restrepo-Ochoa (2015), in their historical analysis of conceptions of mental health, found that that categories of mental health and normality are linked. Based on their analysis of conceptions of mental health from the Middle Ages to present day, they conclude: "What is considered mentally 'healthy' is linked with what is estimated as 'normal' in every historical and cultural context" (p. 37). They propose four meanings of normality, manifested in the various definitions of mental health: health/illness, statistical normality/statistical abnormality, well-being/discomfort, and adjustment/maladjustment. While Jaramillo and Restrepo-Ochoa provide a dispassionate perspective on normality, Jahoda's (1958) approach rejected these four concepts describing normality as criteria for constructing a definition for mental health.

Jahoda's Positive Mental Health

After criticizing the use of three commonly accepted criteria used to define mental health (absence of mental illness, well-being, and normality), Jahoda (1958) presented her analysis of other, more promising concepts used to define mental health. She drew upon the works of well-known theorists, such as, Freud, Allport, Maslow, Erikson and Rogers to discuss the criteria they used to define mental health. [For a detailed presentation of the concepts and authors associated with them see Jahoda (1958) pp. 22-64]. Of particular interest were concepts deemed promising to define what she termed *"positive* mental health (Jahoda, 1958, p. 23, italics added). The addition of "positive" was likely intended to emphatically disconnect *mental health* from its association with the *absence of illness*.

Jahoda organized relevant concepts extracted from her literature review into six categories: attitude toward the self; growth, development, and self-actualization; integration; autonomy; perception of reality; and environmental mastery. Table 12 presents the categories and their main concepts.

Table 12. Jahoda's Categories of Concepts as Promising Criteria for Positive Mental Health

Categories	Concepts
Attitudes toward the self	• Self-acceptance • Self-confidence • Self-reliance • Self awareness
Growth, development, and self-actualization	• Growth motivation • Self-actualization
Integration	• Psychic Balance • Unifying philosophy of life • Resistance to stress

Categories	Concepts
Autonomy	• Independence from social influence • Inner regulation • Internal organization of values, beliefs, and needs • Adjustment and maladjustment to societal norms
Perception of reality	• Perception free from need-distortion • Testing perceptions • Empathy
Environmental mastery	• Ability to love • Adequacy in relationships and work • Efficiency in meeting situational requirement • Appropriate functioning in social roles • Problem solving

Attitudes toward the self, includes concepts such as self-acceptance, self-confidence, self-reliance, and self-awareness. Self-acceptance implies that a person has learned to live with oneself, accepting both inherent strengths and limitations. Related terms (self-confidence, self-esteem, and self-respect) represent positive evaluations of self, meaning that overall, individuals perceive themselves as competent, strong, and generally good people. Self-reliance, another concept in this category, adds a sense of independence from the social environment, as well as internal motivation to the idea of self-confidence. We know that such 'self' concepts, take time to develop fully. Therefore, as criteria for mental health, these concepts may be better applicable to mental health in adulthood, rather than childhood or adolescence.

Growth, development, and self-actualization refer to motivation to achieve positive goals that are higher than simple satisfaction of basic drives and needs. For this category, Jahoda focused mainly on Maslow's *self-actualization*. Given the popularity of *self-actualization*, it is not necessary to discuss the concept in detail to present Jahoda's application of it to mental health. Though the term is generally associated with Maslow, Jahoda noted that *self-actualization* likely originated with Goldstein and was used by others such as Carl Rogers. In her analysis, Jahoda distinguished the two historical conceptions of the term. For Goldstein, self-actualization is a universal human motivation: "There is only one motive by which human activity is set going: the tendency to actualize oneself" (Goldstein, 1940, cited in Jahoda, 1958, p. 31). As such, Goldstein's self-actualization is not considered a criterion for mental health—Jahoda deemed it simply a general principle of life. On the other hand, Jahoda noted that Maslow's theory, in part, contained a criterion for positive mental health. Maslow (1970) distinguished between two types of motivation: deficiency and growth. Deficiency motivation serves to satisfy basic needs such that it "avoids illness but does not yet create positive mental health" (Jahoda, 1958, p. 33). *Growth* motivation—the force triggering self-actualization—is the critical mechanism related to positive mental health.

Integration consists of a balance of psychic forces, unifying philosophy of life and resistance to stress. Balance of psychic forces is discussed in the psychoanalytic tradition, referring to the quality of interaction between ego, id, and superego, rather than simply having the ego as a dominant force. For Jahoda, balance among the three aspects of personality is flexible: at times the ego is dominant, at other times it is the superego or the id (which differs from Freud's concept of ego dominance). Another form of psychic balance concerns relations between unconscious, preconscious and conscious forces, where the role of the unconscious is minimized. The balance of *integration* occurs at the cognitive level, reflected in "a unifying philosophy of life which shapes feelings and behaviors" (Hankin, 2021, par. 5). The final concept in the category of integration is resistance to stress. Unhappiness, anxiety, and stress are universally experienced. Resistance to stress does not mean being immune to stress: stress is not the absence of these negative emotions. It is rather that such experiences do not "seriously unbalance the degree of integration an individual has achieved" (Jahoda, 1958, p. 42).

Autonomy refers to an individual's degree of independence from social influence. Regulation of behavior from within includes (the development of) self-determining attitudes and a growing independence from the outside world—inner regulation replaces fear from imbalance with the social environment. But autonomy is not simply a reaction to anxiety; it is manifested as a force from within individuals, demonstrating the internal organization of values, beliefs, needs and so forth, that comprise a unified philosophy of life. Included in Jahoda's review of the concept of autonomy is Riesman's (1950, cited by Jahoda), who raised the matter of adjustment/maladjustment to societal norms. Autonomous individuals are those who decide whether to conform or not, implying that they might surrender to societal demands, or they might resist.

Perception of reality refers to accuracy of perception of external physical and social reality. Jahoda sidestepped philosophical discourses on reality, because in her view, external reality exists. In healthy individuals, perception is anchored to reality, but it is also unique to an individual. Jahoda argued against using *correct* with respect to perception: she preferred *relative freedom from need-distortion*. Such freedom creates healthy perception, which is "…a process of viewing the world so that one is able to take in matters one wishes were different, without distorting them to fit these wishes" (p. 51). Individuals lacking in mental health simply reject reality if it is discrepant from their needs and wishes, or if reality causes anxiety.

Perception that is free from need-distortion is particularly important in social interactions. Freedom from need-distortion forms the basis of effectiveness in relationships by *facilitating empathy, interpersonal competence, and social sensitivity*. Empathy, for example requires putting aside one's needs, and focusing on the other person's needs with the intent of understanding their experiences, including their emotions. Interpersonal effectiveness is based on accurate perception of the inner states of other people, which is facilitated by a lack of focus on one's own needs.

Environmental mastery, Jahoda's sixth and final category, includes several concepts: ability to love; adequacy in love, work, and play; efficiency in meeting situational requirements; capacity for adaptation and adjustment; and efficiency in problem solving. *Love* includes success in romantic and sexual relationships. *Meeting situational requirements* includes understanding and engaging with the social roles of other individuals. Implicit in meeting situational requirements are the processes of adaptation and adjustment, as Hankin (2021) states:

> *Mastery of the environment refers to achieving success in some social roles and appropriate function in those roles. Positive mental health also includes the ability to have positive affective interpersonal relations. The social roles involved in environmental mastery may include sexual partner, parent, and worker. Environmental mastery suggests the ability to adapt, adjust, and solve problems in an efficient manner.* (para 8)

Building Blocks Not Definitions. It is important to note that the concepts Jahoda presented are *not* her definition of positive mental health: they are a set of building blocks recommended for constructing definitions of mental health. "Definitions" is plural because conceptions of mental health must take cultural differences into account. Jahoda rejected the notion of a single definition of mental health because of cultural diversity. In creating culturally appropriate definitions, actual concepts will vary. For example, if a particular culture does not value individuality, concepts in the *attitude toward self* category should be omitted. Regardless of the composition of multiple criteria of definition, Jahoda stated that *positive mental health* would indicate having met all the criteria included in a particular definition. Jahoda provided an example of the multi-criterion approach by stating her preferred categories: "active adjustment (environmental mastery), integration, and perception as jointly constituting mental health" (Jahoda, 1958, p. 71).

Jahoda's Categories and Current Definitions of Mental Health

Jahoda's critique of common approaches to mental health and her six categories are visible in current definitions of mental health. Table 13 presents current definitions from international organizations concerned with mental health. Consistent with Jahoda's critique of concepts used to define mental health, there are no references in these modern definitions to *absence of mental illness* and *normality*. Well-being is an obvious exception. *Well-being* appears to be a universal component of current definitions, which we can surmise that Jahoda would criticize. In contrast, all definitions contain one or more the concepts that constitute her six categories.

Table 13. A Sample of International Definitions of Mental Health and Jahoda's Categories

Organization	Mental Health Definition	Jahoda's Categories
Canadian Mental Health Association https://cmha.ca/blogs/mental-health-what-is-it-really	Mental health is a state of well-being, and we all have it. Just like we each have a state of physical health, we also each have our mental health to look after. It's not just about surviving, it's about thriving. It's enjoying life, having a sense of purpose, and being able to manage life's highs and lows. Good mental health includes: 1. A sense of purpose 2. Strong relationships 3. Feeling connected to others 4. Having a good sense of self 5. Coping with stress 6. Enjoying life	• Environmental mastery • Integration • Environmental mastery • Environmental mastery • Attitudes toward the self • Integration
National Institute of Mental Health (USA) https://medlineplus.gov/mentalhealth.html	Mental health includes our emotional, psychological, and social well-being. It affects how we think, feel, and act as we cope with life. It also helps determine how we handle stress, relate to others, and make choices. Mental health is important at every stage of life, rom childhood and adolescence through adulthood and aging.	• Integration • Environmental mastery
Singapore Association for Mental Health What is Mental Wellness | Singapore Association for Mental Health: Mental Wellness for All (samhealth.org.sg)	Mentally well people are positive, self-assured, and happy. They are in control of their thoughts, emotions, and behaviour. This enables them to handle challenges, build strong relationships and enjoy life. Achieving good mental health will enable you to: • Realise your own abilities • Cope with the stress and challenges of life • Engage in productive work • Contribute to your community	• Environmental mastery • • Growth, Development, Self-actualization • Integration • Environmental mastery

Organization	Mental Health Definition	Jahoda's Categories
World Health Organization https://www.who.int/mental_health/evidence/en/promoting_mhh.pdf	Mental health is a state of well-being in which an individual realizes his or her own abilities, can cope with the normal stresses of life, can work productively and is capable to make contributions to his or her community.	• Growth, Development, Self-actualization • Integration • Environmental mastery

It is one thing to match Jahoda's categories to current mental health definitions; it is another to state with authority that Jahoda inspired them. Only WHO (World Health Organization, 2004) refers explicitly to Jahoda's definition, indicating her influence:

> *Jahoda (1958) elaborated on the 1947 WHO declaration that "health is not merely the absence of illness but a complete state of physical, psychological and social well-being" by separating mental health into three domains. First, mental health involves self-realization in that individuals are allowed to fully exploit their potential. Second, mental health includes a sense of mastery by the individual over their environment, and, finally, that positive mental health also means autonomy, as in individuals having the ability to identify, confront, and solve problems. (p. 20)*

More recently, the Committee on Ethical Issues of the European Psychiatric Association, though critical of Jahoda's definition, apparently agreed with her critique of using well-being as a criterion for mental health, though for different reasons. Referring specifically to the WHO definition, Galderisi et al., (2015) state that it is difficult to conceive of well-being as a key aspect of mental health with many situations in life, for example, when an individual feels well-being after committing a heinous crime. Conversely, it would be considered healthy for a person to feel desperation if that person were fired from a job when opportunities for employment were scarce. While others reject well-being as part of the definition, they do accept that definitions need to be as culturally neutral as possible. Galderisi et al (2015) propose the following definition:

> *Mental health is a dynamic state of internal equilibrium which enables individuals to use their abilities in harmony with universal values of society. Basic cognitive and social skills; ability to recognize, express and modulate one's own emotions, as well as empathize with others; flexibility and ability to cope with adverse life events and function in social roles; and harmonious relationship between body and mind represent important components of mental health which contribute, to varying degrees, to the state of internal equilibrium.* (Italics in original, p.231-232)

There are some general similarities with Jahoda's categories and the above definition. Of particular interest is "harmony with the universal values of society" which is similar to Jahoda's *adjustment to society*, though reference to universal values is novel. Universal values include "respect and care for oneself and other living beings; recognition of connectedness between people; respect for the environment; respect for one's own and others' freedom" (p. 232). The inclusion of adherence to universal values as a criterion for mental health, ironically, magnifies the positive dimension of mental health far more than the notion of well-being.

Summary. Jahoda (1958) criticized the common criteria used in her day to define mental illness and proposed alternate criteria to define positive mental health. She rejected the criterion *mental health as the absence of mental illness* because mental illness itself is poorly defined. More importantly, mental illness is culturally-bound—behavior that constitute illness in one society may be perceived as healthy in another. *Normality*, with its dual but related meanings of statistical and prescriptive, and *well-being*, are rejected. Rejection of *well-being* is noteworthy, because she rejected it on the grounds that, its descriptors, such as happiness and satisfaction, are vague terms. Interestingly, *well-being* appears as a criterion of mental health in a sample of international definitions.

Based on her review of extant psychological research of her time, Jahoda proposed more suitable criteria for definitions of mental health. Proposed criteria were based on a thorough review of literature, identifying concepts defined by established authors' conceptions of mental health. Jahoda organized the various concepts into six categories: attitude toward the self; growth, development, and self-actualization; integration; autonomy, perception of reality; and environmental mastery. To consider cultural diversity globally (between countries) and locally (within countries), Jahoda suggested abandoning the goal of a universal definition of mental health. Instead, she proposed the use of the above-named concepts to develop various definitions of mental health which reflect population diversity.

Definitions of mental health by selected international organizations were compared with Jahoda's categories. While Jahoda's concepts can be recognized in the various definitions, it is only WHO that documented the influence of Jahoda on its definition. There is a notable exception—despite Jahoda's critique of *well-being*, that phrase has become a universal synonym for mental health.

Dąbrowskian Mental Health and Jahoda's Positive Mental Health

In Dąbrowski's discussions of mental health (Dąbrowski, 1964, 1970), like Jahoda he rejects the three approaches to defining mental health (normality, well-being, and absence of mental illness), but his rationale differs. Normality is criticized because it is determined by the frequency of human characteristics and behaviors that is prevalent in society. A sample of the most frequent, and therefore normal, characteristics include: practical rather than theoretical intelligence, egocentric rather than other-oriented attitudes towards people, compliance with group thinking and behavior, and preponderance of self-preservation and sexual instincts. Dąbrowski is adamant in his rejection of normality:

> *Such a group of normal traits in a person should, according to many, allow us to describe him [or her] as mentally healthy. Can we agree? No. This formulation is humiliating to mankind [humankind]; a more suitable definition of mental health must contain, besides average values, exemplary ones* (Dąbrowski, 1964, p. 113).

Well-being as a criterion of mental health was tersely dismissed by Dąbrowski. "The concept of mental health based on psychic well-being is clearly erroneous. Fairly stable feelings of well-being are characteristic of psychopaths, patients with general paralysis, and some cases of organic brain damage" (Dąbrowski, 1970, pp. 56-57). Mental health as the absence of mental illness is rejected not because *mental illness* is a vague term, but rather on theoretical grounds. In the theory of positive disintegration, *states of anxiety, depression and other symptoms of mental illness are necessary conditions for positive development*. Counterintuitively, mental *illness* is often defined is a "symptom" of Dąbrowskian mental *health*.

The similarity between Jahoda's and Dąbrowski's perspectives ends with the criticism of the three concepts used to define mental health (normality, well-being, and absence of mental illness). Some of Jahoda's concepts are simply incompatible with the theory of positive disintegration; other concepts are lexically identical but are different in meaning. Jahoda's *integration, perception of reality*, and *adjustment* are inconsistent with the theory. From a Dąbrowskian point of view, Jahoda's integration is a unilevel construct. Integration includes achieving a state of balance among psychic forces, such as Freud's tripartite personality structure. For her, integration also includes resistance to stress, meaning that negative experiences do not "seriously unbalance" an individual's equilibrium. In contrast, in the theory of positive disintegration, integration has both a negative and a positive meaning, as expressed in two levels of development: primary and secondary integration. Furthermore, a "seriously unbalanced" state—positive disintegration—is required for advanced development. Perception of reality typically refers to accuracy of perception, determined by the degree to which it is anchored to external reality and free from distortion by needs. Jahoda's view of perception and its relation to positive mental health are inconsistent with aspects of Dabrowskian development. As Mika (2008) notes:

> *[Dąbrowski] stressed the importance of imagination and intuition in accelerated development, saying that many internal processes—which may be only loosely or not at*

all based on reality, such as hunches, dreams, imaginary projects and plans, inner doubts, conflicts, excitations, and inhibitions—awaken our creativity and the need for discovery and innovation. (pp. 142-143)

Adjustment and adaptation to the social environment are concepts included in Jahoda's view of positive mental health. These concepts, part of the environmental mastery category, emphasize the importance of compliance with societal prescriptions. Mentally healthy individuals are those that adhere to societal expectations and its definition of appropriate functioning in social roles. Emphasis on compliance with demands of the social environment is inconsistent with development in the theory of positive disintegration. Generally, Jahoda's environmental mastery category, in Dabrowskian terms, describes adjusting to "what is" rather than to "what ought to be".

Though some of Jahoda's criteria for mental health run counter to the theory of positive disintegration, some of her concepts are found in Dąbrowski's theory. These include self-awareness and self-reliance (attitude toward self); independence from social influence and inner regulation (autonomy); and empathy (perception). These criteria lack the dynamic quality ascribed to them by Dąbrowski—they are simply static descriptors in Jahoda's concept of positive mental health. In the theory of positive disintegration, Dąbrowski explains that these positive criteria develop through the *dynamics* of positive disintegration.

What is Dąbrowskian Mental Health?

Having contrasted Dąbrowski's approaches to Jahoda's criteria of mental health, the question remains: What is mental health according to Dąbrowski? Familiarity with the with the theory of positive disintegration offers a ready answer. In his earliest English language book, the chapter titled "Mental Health as the Progressive Development of Personality" (p. 108, Dąbrowski 1964) provides a cryptic answer to the question. He goes on to explain the implications of the title: "Given a definition of mental health as the development of the personality, we can say that all individuals who present active development in the direction of a higher level of personality (including most psychoneurotic patients) are mentally healthy" (p. 112). In other words, *anyone who is on a Dąbrowskian developmental trajectory is mentally healthy.* The potential for development was emphasized by Dąbrowski in a posthumously published book (translated by Elizabeth Mika). Dąbrowski writes that mental health is "…the capacity for development toward multidimensional understanding, experiencing, discovering, and creating an ever-higher hierarchy of reality and values up to the concrete individual and social ideal" (Dąbrowski, 1996, *In Search of Mental Health*, pp. 22-23 cited in Mika, 2008, p. 150). Clearly, Dąbrowskian mental health is synonymous with the process of development through positive disintegration.

Dąbrowski's definition of mental health is qualitatively different from the sample of definitions provided by international organizations, summarized in Table 12. Recall that the definitions contain concepts proposed by Jahoda. We should expect, then, that some of the terms used in the sample definitions are incompatible with Dąbrowski's definition, while other terms are seen in his theory. *State of well-being* is common to all definitions and yet is rejected by Dąbrowski, as noted earlier. *Positive self-concept* and *hedonism*, which are inconsistent with positive disintegration, are part of some definitions: "having a good sense of self" and "enjoying life" (Canadian Mental Health Association—CMHA) and "mentally healthy people are positive, self-assured, and happy…and enjoy life" (Singapore Association for Mental Health—SAMH). Actualizing potential is a theme among some definitions: "Realizing your own abilities" (SAMH); "realizes his or her own abilities" (World Health Organization—WHO). Dąbrowski rejected *self-actualization* as being too self-focused to be developmentally significant. *Being productive* is also emphasized in some definitions: "engages in productive work" (SAMH); "can work productively" (WHO). *Creative productivity* is part of Dąbrowski's approach, but productivity itself may be a sign of one-sided development, rather than mental health. In contrast, the sample of definitions also include several terms that may be compatible with Dąbrowski's perspective: "sense of purpose" and "feeling connected to others" (CMHA); "contribution to your community" (SAMHA); "make contributions to his or her community" (WHO). However, despite any overlap in terminology between current definitions, Jahoda's categories and the theory of positive disintegration, Dąbrowskian mental health applies only to those who have achieved advanced development or have the potential to do so.

As with other psychological constructs, the theory of positive disintegration reframes mental health. The reconsideration of the construct does contain some similarity with other definitions and could possibly be viewed e as a form of *positive mental health*. However, similarity with other definitions is superficial; conceptually, Dąbrowski's approach is qualitatively different.

For Dąbrowski, mentally healthy individuals are those who experience positive disintegration. This is not limited to those who achieve secondary integration (Level V), but also includes individuals who are in the process of development. The implication is that individuals at primary integration (Level I) are not mentally healthy, while those in the throes of spontaneous multilevel disintegration (Level III) are. The latter statement explains the degree to which Dąbrowski's view diverges from the generally accepted view of mental illness and mental health. Dynamisms of Level III produce anxiety, depression, and inner conflict, essential for development (i.e., mental health). But those experiences are deemed symptoms (i.e., mental illness) in traditional psychiatry. Concerning individuals at primary integration who display no symptoms? I wonder whether they are the people Dąbrowski had in mind when he used the phrase "so-called normal".

PART IV:
Concluding Reflections

Chapter 12. Modifications and Elaborations

CHAPTER 12
Modifications and Elaborations

In the preface of "Mental Growth Through Positive Disintegration", Dąbrowski writes: "The author [Dąbrowski] is convinced that the majority of problems and hypotheses presented here will undergo substantial modification. He [Dąbrowski] will appreciate it as an expression of the fact that this theory is 'alive'..." (Dąbrowski, 1970, p. xi).

Reading those few words makes it clear that Dąbrowski understood that the death knell of a theory is a lack of scrutiny and subsequent refinement. Accepting a theory without full examination is a form of neglect which will lead to its atrophy. Testing hypotheses and close inspection of constructs are processes that breathe fresh air into a theory, thereby keeping it alive. Currently there is virtually no testing of Dąbrowski's hypotheses, and researchers seem fixated on but one of his constructs: overexcitability. As a theoretical psychologist, I am not interested in conducting empirical investigations, though I have spent a great deal of energy urging research psychologists to examine the full scope of the theory. Testing Dąbrowski's hypotheses, and not just endlessly pursuing correlations of overexcitability and giftedness, would honor Dąbrowski's wish to keep his theory alive. I have explored the possibility that the theory may need substantial modification through careful review of the original, and consideration of it in contrast with other psychological theories and with my experience as a psychotherapist.

After years of study, scrutiny, and reflection, I believe that the theory of positive disintegration does not need a substantial reformulation of its core concepts and propositions. The theory does need some refinements, in the form of clarifications and elaborations. I propose clarifications of the ideas of *developmental potential* and *levels of development*, and elaborations of *self and self-concept, emotion, intelligence*, and *mental health*. These proposed refinements do not contradict or question basic tenets of the theory. To put it another way, what follows is *not* a *Neo*-Dąbrowskian perspective; I have been an advocate of his theory, and I remain a 'dyed-in-the-wool' Dąbrowskian.

Modifications: Developmental Potential and Levels of Development

Developmental Potential. Developmental potential is a triple-faceted construct composed of overexcitability, special abilities and talents, and the third factor (autonomy). I argue that developmental potential should be defined solely by multifaceted overexcitability, see Figure 14.

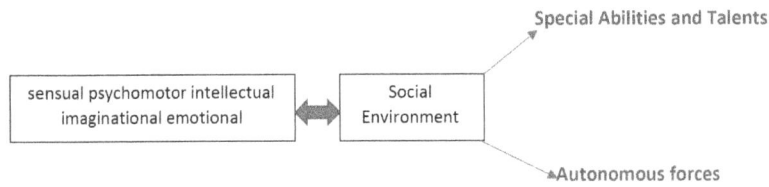

Figure 14. Five Forms of Overexcitability as Developmental Potential

I propose this refinement for two reasons. Developmental potential is an inherited characteristic; of its three constituents, only overexcitability is described as heritable. Special abilities and talents, in my opinion, are not strictly heritable traits. Special abilities and talents are the product of inherited potential interacting with the social environment; they represent extraordinary achievement. Underlying this perspective is the view that abilities and talents do not represent *potential* for prodigious achievement but rather *actual extraordinary achievement*. It is the interaction of the five forms of overexcitability, particularly intellectual and imaginational, which under certain environmental conditions, is responsible for the "special abilities and talents".

A rationale for removing the third factor from the definition of developmental potential is found in the theory itself. Technically, that component of the definition of developmental potential is embedded in a general factor: "autonomous inner forces, particularly, the third factor." The latter phrase states that the third factor is one of Dąbrowski's dynamisms, an important example of "autonomous inner forces", which defines dynamisms. My interpretation of developmental potential is that it is inherited, implying that all components of it are present at birth. However, the theory explains that dynamisms arise from the interaction of the forms of overexcitability with the social environment—their nuclei reside in overexcitability from birth. In addition, to the third factor, deemed to be a dynamism, a component of developmental potential, it refers to a type of development. The third factor, in contrast to the first and second factors, represents a qualitatively different and higher form of development. Unlike the first factor (biology) and the second factor (environment), the third factor creates autonomous development. In short, the third factor serves three functions in the theory: a part of developmental potential, a super-dynamism serving to co-ordinate other dynamisms of organized multilevel disintegration (Level IV), and a factor of development. Removing the third factor from the definition of developmental potential streamlines its important function in the theory.

I have found some support for my suggestion in Dąbrowski's comment about overexcitability and developmental potential. He stated that overexcitability is the best measure of developmental potential.

Levels of Development. I propose modifications relating to Levels III and IV and removing primary integration from the Levels altogether.

Level III Composed of Disintegrating Dynamisms. Level III, spontaneous multilevel disintegration, is the disintegration part of positive disintegration, laying the foundation for its transformation part, represented by Level IV, organized multilevel disintegration. Development does not proceed by "fully accomplishing" Level III, followed by Level IV it is far more complicated. We are interested in the *conceptualization* of Level III, not on how it is experienced. Conceptually, I suggest that only the disintegrating dynamisms should be listed in that Level. The implication is that positive maladjustment, hierarchization and creativity (creative instinct) be reassigned to Level IV because, they are not disintegrating, but rather developmental dynamisms. That would leave what we call "self-dynamisms" (technically the disintegrating self-dynamisms): astonishment with oneself, disquietude with oneself, feelings of shame, feelings of guilt, and dissatisfaction with oneself in Level III.

Renaming Level IV. Level IV (organized multilevel disintegration) should be renamed. Dąbrowski himself used the word "unified" to describe this Level, in a table of levels and dynamisms (Dąbrowski, 1996, p. 31). More to the point, in a discussion of Level IV he states: "Its main characteristics are conscious shaping and synthesis. At this level a person exhibits more tranquility, systematization, and conscious transformation" (1996, p. 19). Using "multilevel disintegration" does not accurately reflect the nature of this Level. I propose *multilevel resolution*; it more closely aligns with Dąbrowski's conception.

Primary Integration and Four levels of Development. As I argued in Chapter 5, primary integration should be removed as a level of *development*. Dąbrowski himself used "adevelopmental"—a lack of development—to describe this first level. To be clear, I am not suggesting eliminating the concept of primary integration—it is a *critical component* of the theory. The other four levels describe the process and achievement of advanced development. Removal of primary integration from the levels seems consistent with its description in the theory.

Disengagement of primary integration from the levels contributes to a reconfiguration of the usual, hierarchical representation of the levels. Dąbrowski was quite emphatic that his theory was not a typical stage theory, and that progression through the levels was not linear, not sequential. He cautioned against the use of "transition" to denote movement through the levels. Current graphic representations of the levels, with their explanatory texts, convey the impression that his theory is a typical stage theory: individuals begin with the level of primary integration proceed to unilevel disintegration, apparently leaving primary integration behind, then on to spontaneous multilevel disintegration, organized multilevel disintegration and, finally secondary integration. Such a presentation is similar to the presentation of typical stage theories such as Piaget and Erikson (see Table 6 p. 80).

Primary integration (Level I) functioning does not disappear with the rise of unilevel disintegration (Level II), nor with the onset of spontaneous multilevel disintegration (Level III). If primary integration vanished with the rise of Level II, there would be no need for Level III. In fact, the operation of primary integration is evident in Level III. The disintegrating dynamisms imply the co-existence of the rigid mental organization of Level I. Feelings of shame, guilt and dissatisfaction with self cannot occur unless individuals become aware that they are functioning (i.e., thinking or behaving) at a primitive level, thereby experiencing, for example, shame or guilt. Therefore, primary integration functioning must continue into Level III.

I understand why a table is used to represent the levels because it is challenging to represent the intricate dynamics of Dąbrowskian development in two-dimensional space. In addition, including primary integration as a first level of development creates an interesting symmetry with secondary integration as the final level. However, in my opinion, there are conceptual challenges created by both the intricate dynamics and the Level I-Level V symmetry. My attempt to address those challenges is seen in Figure 15.

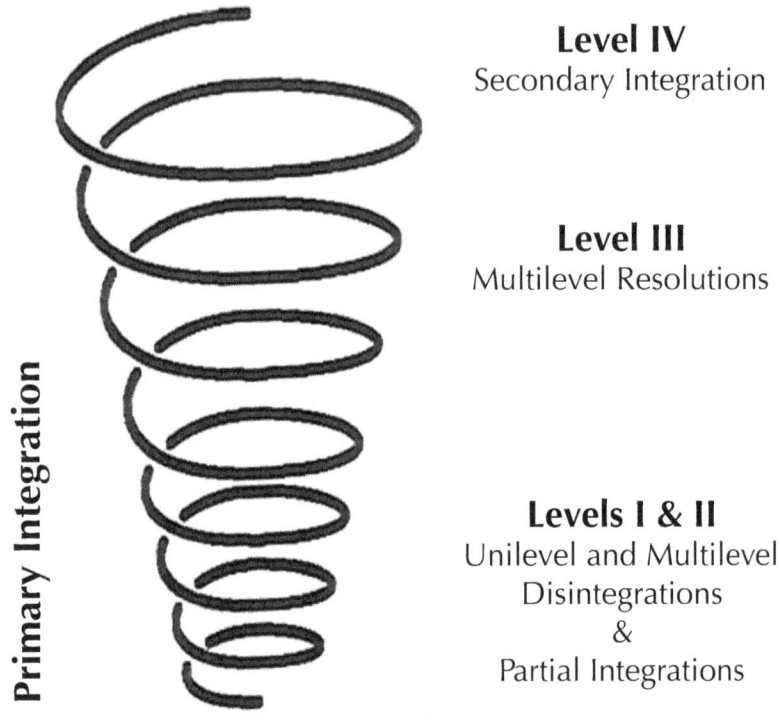

Figure 15. Primary Integration and Four Levels of Development

The spiral represents the progression from primary to secondary integration. Primary integration, on the left side of the spiral is deliberately located such that parts of it are below the spiral. That is intended to indicate the existence of primary integration prior to the appearance of dynamisms. The lower, narrow end of the spiral represents the rigid mental organization of primary integration; the higher wider part represents the broader mental functioning of the process of development. The spiral depicts the interplay of disintegrating dynamisms and primary integration drives and needs. The disintegrating dynamisms of Levels I and II, unilevel and multilevel disintegration respectively, work to gradually destroy primary integration functioning. The results of their work are countless partial integrations until all vestiges of primary integration are destroyed, replaced by the developmental dynamisms of Level III, multilevel resolution, nearing the top of the spiral. With the action of dynamisms such as subject object in oneself, education of oneself, autopsychotherapy, authentism and the third factor, development progresses to Level IV, secondary integration. I think that Figure 15 is a better visual approximation of the levels of development in the theory of positive disintegration than a tabular representation. However, I do not claim that it does justice to the ebb and flow of development as Dąbrowski envisioned it.

Elaborations of Constructs

Self and Self-Concept, Emotion, Intelligence, and Mental Health

Self. Self appears countless times in the theory of positive disintegration and therefore its meaning should be clarified. It is not uncommon in psychology to distinguish between *self as subject* and *self as object*. Some developmental dynamisms implicitly make that distinction. Self-control suggests self as subject; self-awareness suggests self as object. *Self-object* in oneself implies a dialogue between the two forms of self.

Related to but distinct from *self* is *self-concept*. As I indicated in Chapter 8, self-concept is not found in the theory of positive disintegration. However, self-concept is a mainstream psychological construct that is of great interest to both professionals and the public. Given its popularity, I suggest that including an analysis of it in the theory of positive disintegration could be beneficial to the theory. Consideration of self-concept may add another, perhaps more accessible, way to help people appreciate the process of Dabrowskian development. As I see it, self-concept, with its evaluative form, self-esteem, would be in primary integration, as part of normal development. Since both concepts are products of the social environment (second factor), they are therefore considered lower cognitive structures. Positive disintegration would destroy them and replace both by a higher cognitive structure that I have called *authentic autonomous self (see Chapter 8)*. Advanced development, then, could be described as a progression from self-concept/self-esteem to the creation of one's authentic self.

Emotion. Since the concept of emotions occupies a prominent position in the theory of positive disintegration, it requires a focused theory for explication. I suggest that the social-cognitive model of emotion underlies how *it* is construed in the theory of positive disintegration for two reasons. First, the social-cognitive model explains how emotions arise, which is currently lacking in the theory. Emotions are created through individuals' appraisal of events. Second, the cognitive process of appraisal, explains the differentiation between "lower" and "higher emotions", a phrase often used by Dąbrowski. Primitive cognition includes primitive or unilevel appraisals of events leading to lower emotions. With mental growth, appraisals of events become more complex and multilevel resulting in the Dąbrowskian higher level emotions.

Intelligence. It is clear that Dąbrowski espoused Wechsler's approach to intelligence, though it is not explicitly stated in the texts. "Intelligence" is ubiquitous in the theory and so it seems that an explicit conception of the construct would be beneficial, especially because Dąbrowski differentiates intelligence from intellectual overexcitability. Such distinction begs questions, for example, does intellectual overexcitability subsume a high level of intelligence? A precise definition of intelligence will assist in clarifying the difference between *intelligence* and *intellectual overexcitability*. I suggest that intelligence be defined as Wechsler's *general intelligence* and that it is subsumed under *intellectual overexcitability*.

Mental health. Aronson, the force behind the publication of Positive Disintegration (Dąbrowski, 1964) pointedly stated that the most significant of Dąbrowski's contributions was the reframing of psychopathology and mental health. The reconceptualization of mental health is made clear by Dąbrowski's reserving the term for those individuals who are on a Dąbrowskian growth trajectory. From that perspective, there are relatively few individuals in a population to whom the phrase would apply (who are in fact mentally healthy). That only a small proportion of a population is technically considered mentally healthy is not unique to its conception in Dąbrowski's theory. Very few individuals would be included if we applied, for example, all the criteria contained in the World Health Organization's (WHO) definition (see Chapter 11). Clarification regarding mental health is needed because Dąbrowski's and current definitions require that we designate those individuals who do NOT meet the definitions. The question is not simply a matter of semantics—if we are not mentally healthy, then what are we? Dąbrowski would likely call us "so-called normal". For Dąbrowski, then, there are two categories: *normal* and *mentally healthy*. In other words, primary integrated is *normal,* and *developing* is *mentally healthy.* As noted in Chapter 5, primary integration includes subcategories of normality and psychopathy. Therefore, I propose the following Dąbrowskian terminology in response to the above question: psychopathy, normality, and mental health. If we are not in the development with its psychoneuroses, we are likely normal, since psychopathy can be attributed to only a small fraction of a population.

My Final Word

Awareness

With all the emphasis on emotions in the theory of positive disintegration, it is easy to forget that the transformations in development are, in fact, the products of mental growth. There is no question that emotions are central to the theory; however, it is cognition that produces them. How situations and the behavior of individuals are appraised determines the emotions that are experienced. This is readily apparent from the perspective of the social-cognitive theory of emotions: the quality of appraisals determines the type of emotions produced. Appraisal, as a cognitive process, is affected by an individual's mental development. Constituents of appraisal include such factors as intelligence and self-efficacy. When considered in a Dąbrowskian context, forms of overexcitability must be included as influential factors in the process of appraisal. Overexcitability enables multilevel perception and a cognitive processing of events, representing an integral part of the appraisal process. Thus, individuals characterized by multilevelness will, as part of their thorough appraisal of social situations, experience higher emotions (e.g., compassion) than those individuals with a unilevel understanding, who will experience lower emotions (e.g., disinterest). The difference lies in the quality of mental growth.

When I reflect on the role of cognition in advanced development, I believe that the essential mental ability is awareness. It is impossible to overemphasize the importance of *awareness* in understanding how individuals generally function in daily life. In short, some people notice more details in their surroundings than others. The difference is particularly applicable in social situations. In Dąbrowski's theory, level of awareness makes the core distinction between unilevel and multilevel experiences of reality. Understanding the difference between low and heightened awareness, rather than emotion, is critical to fully appreciating Dąbrowski's explanation of the unfolding of development.

References

Aavik, T., & Dobewall, H. (2017). Where is the location of "Health" in the human values System? Evidence from Estonia. Social Indicators Research, 131(3), 1145–1162. https://doi-org.ezproxy.lib.ucalgary.ca/10.1007/s11205-016-1287-4

American Psychiatric Association. (2013). Diagnostic and statistical manual of mental disorders (5th ed.). Arlington, VA: American Psychiatric Publishing.

Blanch, A. (2015). Evaluating fluid and crystallized abilities in the performance of an educational process. *Instructional Science, 43*(3), 427-442.

Brown, R.E. (2016). Hebb and Cattell: The genesis of the theory of fluid and crystallized intelligence, Frontiers in Human Neuroscience, 10, p. 606.

Cattell, R.B. (1943). The measurement of adult intelligence, Psychological Bulletin, 40, 153-193.

Cattell, R.B. (1971). *Abilities: Their structure growth and action.* Boston: Houghton Mifflin.

Cooley, C. H. (1964). *Human nature and the social order.* New York: Schocken. (Original work published 1902).

Conte, F., Costantini, G., Rinaldi, L., Gerosa, T., & Girellie, L. (2020). Intellect is not that expensive: differential association of cultural and socioeconomic factors with crystallized intelligence in a sample of Italian adolescents, Intelligence, 81.101466.

Dąbrowski, K. (1964). *Positive disintegration.* Boston: Little, Brown and Company.

Dąbrowski, K. (1967). *Personality-shaping through positive disintegration.* Boston: Little, Brown and Company.

Dąbrowski, K. (with Kawczak, A., & Piechowski, M. M.). (1970). *Mental growth through positive disintegration*. London: Gryf.

Dąbrowski, K. (1972). *Psychoneurosis is not an illness*. London: Gryf.

Dąbrowski, K. (with Kawczak, A., & Sochanska, J.). (1973). *The dynamics of concepts*. London: Gryf.

Dąbrowski, K. (1996a). *Multilevelness of emotional and instinctive functions. Part 1: Theory and description of levels of behavior*. Lublin, Poland: Towarzystwo Naukowe Katolickiego Uniwersytetu Lubelskiego.

Eno, L. (1978). Predicting achievement and the theory of fluid and crystallized intelligence. *Psychological Reports, 43*(3), 847-852.

Finlay, A. K., Wray-Lake, L., Warren, M., & Maggs, J. (2015). Anticipating their future: Adolescent values for the future predict adult behaviors. International Journal of Behavioral Development, 39(4), 359–367.

Flavell, J. H. (1963). *The developmental psychology of Jean Piaget*. NY: Van Nostrand Company.

Galderisi, S., Heinz, A., Kastrup, M., Beezhold, J., & Sartorius, N. (2015). Toward a new definition of mental health, World Psychiatry, 14 (2), 231-233.

Hankin, J. (2021). "Positive Mental Health ." Encyclopedia of Sociology. . *Encyclopedia.com*. **13 Jan. 2021** <https://www.encyclopedia.com>.

Jahoda, M. (1958). Current Concepts of Positive Mental Health: A report to the staff director, Jack R. Ewalt. NY: Basic Books.

James, W. (1990). *The principles of psychology*. New York: Dover. (Original work published 1890).

Jaramillo, J.C. & Restrepo-Ochoa, D.A. (2015). Normality and Mental Health: analysis of a multivalent relationship. *Journal of Psychology CES, 8* (1), 37-46.

Kaufman, A.S., Raiford, S.E., & Coalfon, D.L. (2016). *Intelligence testing with the WISC-V*. NY: John Wiley and Sons Inc.

Kawczak, (1970). Introduction—The methodological structure of the theory of positive disintegration. In K. Dąbrowski. with M.M. Piechowski and Kawczak. London: Gryf, pp. 1-16.

Kaya, F., Juntune, J., & Stough, L. (2015). Intelligence and its relationship to achievement, *Elementary Education,* 14(3)1060-1078, http://dx.doi.org/10.17051/io.2015.25436

Kemper, T.D. (1978). Toward a sociology of emotions: Some problems and some solutions, *The American Sociologist, 13,* 30-41.

Kemper, T.D. (1991). Predicting emotions from social relations, *Social Psychology Quarterly, 54,* 330-342.

Kemper, T. D. (1993). Sociological models in the explanation of emotions. In M. Lewis & J. M. Haviland (Eds.), *Handbook of emotions* (pp. 41-51). New York: Guilford Press.

Kuhn, D. (1979). The Application of Piaget's Theory of Cognitive Development to Education. *Harvard Educational Review, 49,* 340–360. doi: https://doi.org/10.17763/haer.49.3.h70173113k7r618r

L. Genshaft, & P. L. Harrison (Eds.), *Contemporary intellectual assessment: Theories,*

Lazarus, R.S. (1966). Psychological stress and the coping process. New York: McGraw–Hill.

Lazarus, R.S. (1991). Cognition and motivation in emotion, *American Psychologist, 46,* 352-367.

Lazarus, R. S. (1993). From psychological stress to the emotions: A history of changing outlooks, *Annual Review of Psychology, 44,* 1-21.

Lazarus, R. S. (2006) Emotions and interpersonal relationships: Toward a person-centered conceptualization of emotion and coping, Journal of Personality, 74, 9-46.

Martinez, D. (2019). Immediate and long-term memory and their relation to crystallized and fluid intelligence. *Intelligence, 76,* 101382. https://doi.org/10.1016/j.intell.2019.101382

Maslow, A. H. (1970). *Motivation and personality* (2nd ed.). New York: Harper & Row.

Mead, G. H. (1934). *Mind, self, and society.* Chicago: University of Chicago Press.

Mendaglio, S. (Ed), (2008). The theory of positive disintegration. Scottsdale, AZ: Great Potential Press.

Mendaglio, S. & Tillier, W. (1993). Feeling bad can be good: Dąbrowski's theory applied to the gifted. Paper presented at the World Congress for Gifted and Talented Children, Toronto, Ontario, August].

Mika, E. (2008). Dąbrowski's views on mental health. In S. Mendaglio (Ed.) *The theory of positive disintegration*. Scottsdale, AZ: Great Potential Press, pp. 139-153.

Piaget, J. (1957). *Logic and psychology*. NY: Basic Books Inc.

Piaget, J., & Inhelder, B. (1969). *The psychology of the child*. NY: Basic Books Inc.

Pintner, R. (1921). Intelligence and its measurement: A symposium. *Journal of Educational Psychology, 12,* 139–143.

Raimy, V. C. (1948). Self reference in counseling interviews. *Journal of Consulting Psychology, 12*(3), 153–163.

Rogers, C. R. (1961). *On becoming a person*. Boston: Houghton Mifflin.

Rokeach, M. (1968). A theory of organization and change within value-attitude systems, *Journal of Social Issues*, 24, 13-33.

Rokeach, M. (1973). *The nature of human values*. New York: Free Press.

Rosenberg, M. (1989). Self-concept research: A historical overview, *Social Forces*, 68 (1), 34-44.

Salovey, P., & Mayer, J. D. (1990). Emotional Intelligence. Imagination, Cognition and Personality, 9(3), 185–211. https://doi.org/10.2190/DUGG-P24E-52WK-6CDG.

Sattler, J.M. (2001). *Assessment of children* (4th edition). San Diego, CA: Jerome M. Publisher, Inc.

Schneider, W.J., & McGrew, K.S. (2018). The Cattell-Horn-Carroll theory of cognitive abilities. In D.P. Flanagan, & E.M. McDonough (Eds.). Contemporary intellectual assessment (4th ed.): Theories of tests and issues, pp. 73-163. NY: The Guilford Press.

Schroeders, U., Schipolowski, S., Zettler, I., Golle, J., & Wilhelm, O. (2016) Do the smart get smarter? Development of fluid and crystallized intelligence in 3rd grade, *Intelligence*,59, 84-95.

Schwartz, S. H. (1992). Universals in the content and structure of values: Theory and empirical tests in 20 countries. In M. Zanna (Ed.), *Advances in experimental social psychology* (Vol. 25, pp. 1-65). New York: Academic Press.

Schwartz, S. H. (2012). An Overview of the Schwartz Theory of Basic Values. *Online Readings in Psychology and Culture, 2*(1). https://doi.org/10.9707/2307-0919.1116

Siegler, R.S. (1992) The other Alfred Binet, *Developmental Psychology, 28,* 79-190.

Spearman, (1904). General intelligence, objectively determined and measured. *American Journal of Psychology, 15,* 201-293.

Sternberg R. J., Detterman D. K. (1986). *What is intelligence?* Norwood, NJ: Ablex Publishing.

Sullivan, H. S. (1953). *The interpersonal theory of psychiatry.* New York: Norton.

Sun, X., Nancekivell, S., Gelman, S. A., & Shah, P. (2020). Perceptions of the malleability of fluid and crystallized intelligence. *Journal of Experimental Psychology: General, 150,* 815–827.

Terman, L.M. (1916). *The measurement of intelligence.* Boston: Houghton Mifflin and Co.

Thorndike, R.M. (1997). The early history of intelligence testing. In D.P. Flanagan, & K.S. McGrew& P. L. Harrison (Eds.), *Contemporary Intellectual Assessment.* NY: The Guilford Press. Pp. 3-16.

Thorsen, C., Gustafsson, J-E., & Cliffordson, C. (2014). The influence of fluid and crystallized intelligence on the development of knowledge and skills, *British Journal of Educational Psychology, 84,* 556–570.

Thurstone, L.L. (1938). *Primary mental abilities.* Chicago, ILL: University of Chicago Press.

Tillier, W. (2018*). Personality Development through positive disintegration: The work of Kazimerz Dąbrowski.* Anna Maria, FL: Maurice Bassett.

Wallace, H.M., & Tice, D.M. (2012). Reflected appraisals through a 21st–century looking glass. In M. R., Leary, &, J.P. Tangney (Eds.) (2012). *Handbook of self and identity* (2nd Ed.). NY: Guilford Press, pp. 124-140.

Warne, R. T., & Bumingham, C. (2019). Spearman's g Found in 31 Non-Western Nations: Strong Evidence That g Is a Universal Phenomenon. Psychological Bulletin, 145, (3), 237–272.

Wasserman, J.D. (2018). A history of intelligence assessment: The unfinished tapestry. In Flanagan, D.P., & McDonough, E.M. (Eds.)

Contemporary intellectual assessment: Theories, tests and issues (4th edition). NY: Guilford Press.

Wechsler, D. (1944). *The measurement of Adult intelligence* (3rd Ed). Baltimore, MD: Waverly Press.

World Health Organization (2004). Promoting mental health: concepts, emerging evidence, practice (Summary Report). Geneva: World Health Organization.

About the Author

Salvatore "Sal" Mendaglio, PhD, Professor Emeritus, University of Calgary, is a licensed psychologist. Sal received all his education in Canada: a BA in psychology from St. Francis Xavier University (Nova Scotia), a B.Ed. from the Université de Montréal, an M.Ed. in counseling from McGill University (Montreal), and a PhD in counseling psychology from the University of Toronto. While completing his PhD, he obtained an academic appointment with the University of Calgary. During his 45-year career with the University, Sal taught graduate and undergraduate courses in counseling psychology and graduate courses in educational leadership. He supervised a multitude of master's and doctoral students. He held several administrative positions including Chair of the Counseling Psychology program, Assistant Dean of Student Services, Graduate Program Director. Sal, as co-founder, was instrumental in the creation of the Center for Gifted Education at the University of Calgary. In its approximately 20-year operation, the Center provided advocacy for gifted education and support for educators, parents and graduate students interested in giftedness.

Throughout the various phases of his academic life, the one constant was his passion for counseling gifted individuals. Sal's reflective practice led to academic contributions to the field of gifted education including abundant national and international conference presentations as well as numerous publications in academic journals. In his search for a deeper understanding of the challenges that are encountered by clients with high ability and for resources to enhance his counseling effectiveness, Sal encountered Kazimierz Dabrowski's theory of positive disintegration. That event led to a 30-year journey with the theory, during which time it became the major focus of his academic work and counseling practice. Sal's initial publications on the theory were aimed at encouraging the field of education to consider the complexity of Dabrowski's theory when applying it to giftedness. More recently, his efforts have been on positioning the theory in the field of psychology, both as an acknowledgement of Dabrowski's conception of his theory as a theory of personality and to share with psychologists a new perspective on counseling a subset of clients who are gifted. Dabrowski's theory is the feature of Sal's forthcoming books. articulating his model of the psychology of giftedness.

Printed in the USA
CPSIA information can be obtained
at www.ICGtesting.com
CBHW031018150524
8397CB00002B/8